SOCIAL ENTREPRENEURSHIP

A skills approach

Edited by Robert Gunn and Chris Durkin

This edition published in Great Britain in 2010 by

The Policy Press
University of Bristol
Fourth Floor
Beacon House
Queen's Road
Bristol BS8 1QU
UK

t: +44 (0)117 331 4054
f: +44 (0)117 331 4093
tpp-info@bristol.ac.uk
www.policypress.co.uk

North American office:
The Policy Press
c/o International Specialized Books Services
920 NE 58th Avenue, Suite 300
Portland, OR 97213-3786, USA
t: +1 503 287 3093
f: +1 503 280 8832
info@isbs.com

© The Policy Press 2010

British Library Cataloguing in Publication Data
A catalogue record for this book is available from the British Library.

Library of Congress Cataloging-in-Publication Data
A catalog record for this book has been requested.

ISBN 978 1 84742 289 7 paperback
ISBN 978 1 84742 296 5 hardcover

The right of Robert Gunn and Chris Durkin to be identified as editors of this work has been asserted by them in accordance with the 1988 Copyright, Designs and Patents Act.

Cover design by Qube Design Associates, Bristol
Front cover: image kindly supplied by iStockphoto
Printed and bound in Great Britain by TJ International, Padstow

Contents

List of figures, tables and boxes

Figures

Tables

Boxes

Notes on contributors

Richard Bryant is a volunteer with the Bullingdon Community Association. He has been employed as a community worker in Glasgow and Oxford and taught social policy and community development at Ruskin College, Oxford between 1979 and 2006.

Ian Buchanan teaches social work at the University of York. He has also worked in local authority social services as a senior manager. His interest in the third sector comes through his main research interest in participative research with adults with learning difficulties.

Carol Chyau graduated from Harvard Kennedy School's Masters in Public Administration/International Development programme. During the course of her studies at Harvard, Carol worked with the United Nations Development Programme in New York City and Thailand. She completed projects studying information communication technologies in Thailand and growing sustainable business projects in New York. She also studied internet connectivity in rural areas in Cambodia as a World Resources Institute case writer. Carol has also worked in microfinance with EDPYME Edyficar in Lima, Peru. Carol graduated from the University of Pennsylvania's joint-degree Huntsman Program in International Studies and Business. In 2006 she co-founded Ventures in Development, Shokay and Mei Xiang Cheese with Marie Tze Kwan So. The focus of her work is on Shokay operations and production. She is based in Shanghai.

Tim Curtis is a socially entrepreneurial academic. After advising, starting, operating and sitting on the board of a number of social enterprises in Scotland, Tim began investigating them with research on public procurement in the East Midlands and then led a major research programme at the University of Oxford on social enterprise cultures. Now a senior lecturer at the University of Northampton, Tim leads two programmes, one on social enterprise and one on community development at undergraduate and postgraduate level. He continues to write academic papers on his research and is busy starting social enterprises with students and communities in Northamptonshire. He is a social geographer by training and has 15 years' industrial experience.

Chris Durkin is associate director of the Northampton Institute of Urban Affairs based at the University of Northampton. He is a registered social worker and has worked for the National Society for the Prevention of Cruelty to Children and the probation service His interests in social enterprises are linked to community development and stakeholder engagement.

Andrew Ferguson is currently the business, community and enterprise manager for the University of York Careers Service with responsibility for engaging students and employers in all aspects of the enterprise agenda. Andrew joined the University of York in 2001 after working on small- and medium-sized enterprise development projects in the Middle East, Africa and in the former Communist bloc countries. He has since been the director of the York Award (the University's certificate of personal development), the enterprise learning manager for the White Rose Centre for Enterprise and the operations manager for the White Rose Centre for Excellence in Teaching and Learning in Enterprise at York. He recently completed a joint project on behalf of the Cabinet Office with the University of Leeds to develop training materials to enable careers advisers to work more effectively with social entrepreneurs.

Jon Griffith came to social enterprise early. His first ever job (at 16) was with the Co-op (selling electrical goods at the Royal Arsenal Co-operative Society in his home town, Slough), and his father worked for Waitrose (part of the John Lewis Partnership). After university (BA in English Literature), Jon worked for Oxfam and in the youth service before becoming a freelance consultant. He has undertaken qualitative organisational research with the Centre for Institutional Studies at the University of East London since 1983, has taught postgraduate students there since 1990, and from 2001 until 2007 developed and ran the postgraduate programme Social Enterprise: Development and Management. He was a member of a development education cooperative and two housing cooperatives in the 1980s and 1990s, but now owns a flat in Hastings, although jointly with the Co-operative Bank's mortgage arm so his commitment to cooperation remains undiminished.

Robert Gunn is a lecturer in social policy and social work at the University of York. He is a former probation officer and qualified social worker, and was closely associated with third sector organisations in a community development role.

Wray Irwin currently works for the University of Northampton's Enterprising Skills Agency, delivering a range of activities aimed at supporting individuals to become enterprising participants in their communities and contribute to an enterprising culture. His interest in social enterprise goes back to 2000, when, after 17 years in retail banking, he worked for a local authority supporting community groups to take ownership of community facilities and manage them as effective community businesses. He was also one of the founding members of the Golden Sheaf Credit Union in Kettering. As a result of his work within the credit union movement, Wray went on to be agency manager of the Northamptonshire Co-operative Development Agency, a post he held for over five years, supporting formation and growth of over 50 social enterprises, cooperatives and community businesses. During this time Wray was also chair of Social Enterprise East Midlands, and a member of the East Midlands Co-op Council. Wray's interest has always been in the provision of business support to the sector, and has been keen on ensuring that communities and individuals who are looking to social enterprise solutions for the provision of services have access to appropriate and relevant business support. Wray gained a Master of Studies qualification from the University of Cambridge in social enterprise and community development, for which he researched the motivations of social entrepreneurs.

Gladius Kulothungan teaches, researches and facilitates social entrepreneurship in the UK, Europe and Asia. He is a senior lecturer at the University of East London and a visiting professor at Roskilde University, Denmark and SIT Graduate University, Vermont. Gladius has a practitioner background, and in addition to holding senior management positions in the private, public and voluntary sectors, he has set up social enterprises and led them. His research interests include social innovation, organisational development, ethics of economic institutions and social exclusion.

Anthony (Tony) Mendes, director of the Murphy Center for Entrepreneurship at the University of North Texas, is an acclaimed entrepreneurial educator who formerly served as executive director of the Academy for Entrepreneurial Leadership, at the University of Illinois at Urbana-Champaign. In his role with the Academy for Entrepreneurial Leadership, Tony Mendes was responsible for institutionalising entrepreneurship curricula across all academic units. During his tenure at Illinois, the university achieved national status for entrepreneurship education by *Princeton Review* and *Entrepreneur and Fortune* magazines, and the National Consortium of Entrepreneurship Centers. Prior to the University of Illinois, Tony was director of College Initiatives at the Kauffman Foundation, where he managed a programme grant portfolio of US$30 million, serving over 200 colleges and universities. He holds a PhD in psychology from the University of Missouri, Kansas City, and an MBA from Rockhurst University.

Marie Tze Kwan So is the co-founder of Ventures in Development (VID), a non-profit organisation that catalyses creation of social enterprises in the Greater China region. VID believes that social enterprises are a means to bring forth higher levels of economic and social development. Since 2006, Marie and her partner Carol Chyau have founded two social enterprises: Mei Xiang Yak Cheese (www.meixiangcheese.com) and Shokay (www.shokay.com). Marie graduated from Harvard Kennedy School's Masters in Public Administration/ International Development programme, having previously gained a Bachelor in Economics, Engineering and Management Science from Northwestern University. She has worked for the United Nations Development Programme, the Dubai Development and Investment Authority, Procter & Gamble, and Merrill Lynch. She is a recipient of several awards: Echoing Green Fellow 2008, Asia 21 Young Leader 2008, and Asia Society Business in Development 2006 award. She was recently selected as one of the World Economic Forum Global Young Leaders 2009.

Kimberly Sugden is a leader in marketing strategy and brand management within higher education. In her former role, as the associate director of the Academy for Entrepreneurial Leadership at the University of Illinois, Urbana–Champaign, Kimberly was instrumental in building the centre's marketing portfolio from the ground up and generating global brand recognition. As a member of the Academy's leadership team, Kimberly helped develop the co-curricular strategy for embedding entrepreneurship across all disciplines on the Illinois campus. There she managed the Innovation Teams business plan competition, in addition to several international enterprise initiatives for the Academy and the Worldwide Universities Network. Graphic Design USA has honoured Kimberly with six national marketing awards, and her work has been printed in *Newsweek* and *Entrepreneur* magazines. Kimberly is currently at the University of Oxford working for a postgraduate research degree in the Saïd Business School.

Stan Thekaekara is founder director of Just Change (www.justchangeindia. com), a radical trade cooperative that links producers, consumers and investors across the world to work in mutually beneficial and equitable ways. Currently based in South India, Stan has worked for indigenous peoples' rights, community development and social entrepreneurship since the early 1970s. Known for his radical and innovative thinking on development economics, he is frequently invited to lecture at national and international events. His experience in the sector ranges from grass-roots organisations such as ACCORD, which he co-founded to work for the rights of the indigenous peoples, to serving on the boards of various Indian and international charities such as Oxfam GB, as well as working in academia as a former fellow of the Skoll Centre for Social Entrepreneurship at the Saïd Business School, University of Oxford.

Mandy Young is a Corby mother of two and dedicated member of her community striving to improve the lives of young people. In 2002 she was an apprentice hairdresser caring for her son, John, who had suffered with an undiagnosed brain tumour for seven years. Her family life was shattered when her son became the victim of a vicious attack because he had a skateboard. The only way to overcome this devastation was to turn the experience into a positive one. Mandy and John attended a community consultation and the concept of Adrenaline Alley was born (www.adrenalinealley.co.uk). An approach to Rockingham Speedway (Corby) led to donations of land and resources, allowing the project to open indoors in July 2006. Through her vision, award-winning Mandy has created the UK's biggest indoor urban sports centre, with Europe's first 76ft Resi/vert ramp. Mandy continues to develop and grow the social enterprise to provide a purpose-built, world-class centre of excellence for the future.

Acknowledgements

We would like to thank Emily Watt and her colleagues at The Policy Press for all their help and support in the production of this book. We would also like to offer our many thanks to all the contributors for their interest in and commitment to this project and for their forbearance in the production process.

Robert Gunn would like to thank Elizabeth Gunn for her practical and moral support in this latest writing endeavour.

Chris Durkin would like to thank Kathy, Clare, Sean and Paul for their ongoing love, encouragement and support.

Preface

Welcome to *Social entrepreneurship: A skills approach*. This book has been designed as an introduction to the subject of social entrepreneurship and social enterprise and as an exploration of the core skills needed to initiate, design, run and sustain an organisation that aims to meet a specific social need. If you are new to the subject and interested in what social entrepreneurship and social enterprise are, or are studying different forms of organisations and social policy as part of a course, this book has been written with you in mind. It is also designed for anyone who either works in, or is considering setting up an organisation that has to balance a mission to uphold social justice and maintain financial viability.

The inspiration for the book comes from our experience of teaching undergraduates who demonstrate a passion for social justice and change and who are interested in new ways of conceiving and delivering solutions to social needs that have not been addressed by either the state or the private market sectors. Although there are a number of academic books looking at social entrepreneurship and social enterprises, this text is designed to incorporate the theoretical and the practical. It became clear to us in our teaching that there was a need for a book that brings together theory and practice and introduces readers to the realities of developing their own ideas and aspirations for social organisations. It complements the works already available that cover the theory of policy development, management skills and case study research by focusing on the application of knowledge and expertise to real social problems in a practical way. While the policy and theory we use are based on western thought and tradition, we have used case examples from across the globe to emphasise the global aspects of the social enterprise phenomenon. We hope that you find this a useful approach and we would welcome your feedback on this publication and would be very interested to hear of your experiences of social entrepreneurship.

This book has been written at a time of global economic downturn. This recession has led many to question both the make-up and balance of economies, in particular in the UK on the over-reliance on the financial sector. The collapse of large financial institutions and the subsequent rescue of banks and a number of other industries, most notably in the US has given rise to questions about many management theories and the so-called 'Anglo Saxon' or 'neo-liberal' economic models with their emphasis on labour mobility and short-term gain.

Governments are reassessing how to deliver welfare services to increasingly demanding populations affected by social and economic changes – from ageing populations in the western industrialised countries to the developing countries where populations are expanding and need services for an increasingly youthful population. There is also the need to address health and well-being issues such as malaria, HIV and AIDS, obesity, and alcohol and drug misuse. Debates are taking place as to how such services are to be delivered and paid for. What seems clear is that no one organisational model will emerge and each country will respond to need and opportunities in different ways. It is within this rapidly changing context that social enterprises have emerged as organisations that can provide solutions to the needs of diverse societies.

Social entrepreneurs are not confined to welfare provision and operate in all sectors of the economy. Across the world we can see examples of significant social enterprises operating in a variety of sectors, including the Co-operative movement in the UK, Mondragón Corporation in Spain and the Grameen Bank in Bangladesh. The emergence of corporate social responsibility in mainstream business has also led to companies supporting and developing social enterprises. For example, Danone has linked with the Grameen Bank to form Danone Foods Social Business Enterprise. As you will see in this book, return on investment in all sectors is increasingly seen as not merely about profit maximisation but also about social and community impact, in which social return on investment is seen as part of an approach to measuring success.

What will be seen in the book is that social entrepreneurs do not offer universal solutions but respond to issues in innovative and creative ways in response to perceived local need. However, what will also be shown is that having a 'good idea' or a desire to 'do good' is not enough and all social enterprises if they are to survive have to develop commercially and ensure secure finances and funding. The four different case studies we have selected clearly show that defining need and targeting services can improve the lives of individual service users and enhance the communities in which they live. What these case studies also show is that they are businesses that are affected by the markets within which they operate.

Robert Gunn and Chris Durkin 2010

ONE

Introduction

Robert Gunn and Chris Durkin

The book is laid out in three parts. Part One: Skills in Policy Analysis provides an overview of the policy context that has brought social enterprise to the forefront of UK government policy. It also defines social entrepreneurship and social enterprise. Part Two: Skills for Social Entrepreneurship, looks at the key skills social entrepreneurs need to pursue their dreams to build, finance and manage sustainable organisations. This section also looks at the increasing importance of social innovation. Part Three: Skills in Practice, places all of these skills in their applied context and broadens the scope of our exploration to a global level. We focus on individual experiences and smaller organisations directly linked to specific communities by presenting cases studies from the UK, the US, China and India. These studies present the very different perspectives exhibited by social entrepreneurs while also showing the commonalities of problems they all face.

Chapter descriptions

Part One: Skills in policy analysis

In Chapter Two, Ian Buchanan describes the UK policy context which has shaped the development of voluntary and state welfare activities that have emerged during the 20th century. The argument that the state cannot, and maybe should not, meet every welfare need is explored. This theoretical approach gives the reader analytical tools to evaluate material in subsequent chapters, especially those that contain case studies of real organisations. He looks at the ability of social enterprises to address state and market failures and the future and sustainability of this particular form of social organisation. Buchanan's ideas show how the creation of social value for communities is being delivered by organisations that have to balance a social mission with economic sustainability and long term viability.

Gladius Kulothungan explores in Chapter Three what the terms social enterprise and social entrepreneur mean, their genesis and why social enterprises are currently seen as such important organisations. He looks at how innovation can be engendered in them and offers a basic description of the capitalist economic system and why this has led to the decline of the state's delivery of welfare services. The theme of innovation is developed further in Chapter Eight.

Part Two: Skills for social entrepreneurship

In setting up any organisation you have to find out if there is a market for your services or products. Having the tools to evaluate the needs of a particular group of people or community and their potential ability to shape solutions to meet need are key skills for aspiring social entrepreneurs. In Chapter Four, Richard Bryant adopts a community development approach to defining and identifying need and identifies the skills and qualities needed for successful practice. If a social enterprise is to succeed it needs to develop an organisation that is relevant to the needs of a community, the stakeholders that are central to organisational development. This latter issue is looked at in greater depth in the next chapter.

Chapter Five explores what we mean by 'stakeholder' in present-day organisational and management analysis. Chris Durkin and Robert Gunn identify the number of potential stakeholders involved with social enterprises and explore their different perspectives, including what role, if any, a service user can play. They show how a theoretical model of power can help to identify who is exercising influence in an organisation and how this may enable entrepreneurs to maintain their social mission. The importance of evaluation is looked at within the context of service user involvement.

In Chapter Six, Wray Irwin looks at the practicalities of how to finance a social enterprise and explores the issues faced by social entrepreneurs when trying to access finance either to start or grow an organisation. The problems created by the loose definition of this form of organisation, the issues of sustainability and self-financing are also explored. Some basic economic definitions are presented to help the reader analyse critically the different forms of funding available.

While social entrepreneurs may be fired with a vision to improve the social aspects of people's lives, no enterprise will last without secure funding. In Chapter Seven, Andrew Ferguson shows us how to plan and control the financial aspects of a social enterprise. He takes us through the essential skills for understanding how to calculate income and control cash flow so that organisations can ensure that they have the funds available to uphold their core mission.

Tim Curtis in Chapter Eight develops ideas raised in Chapter Three and explores the role of innovation in the development of ideas to address social difficulties. He measures the benefits of this against the potential risks involved. Innovation is a factor that is used to distinguish social enterprises from traditional charities. The ethical dimensions of such an approach are also discussed, as are the practicalities of analysing particular social situations and implementing innovative strategies. 'Wicked issues' are used as a means of exploring the role of innovation in change. Social innovation is now seen as a central aspect for the development of social policy/welfare.

Chapter Nine provides an overview of the theory of leadership and management and then relates these particular skills to social enterprises. Jon Griffith discusses how organisations change over time and how entrepreneurs and managers have to adapt to new challenges. He also discusses the difficulties of evaluating the impact of leadership and management in the shaping of organisations.

Part Three: Skills in practice

The preceding chapters explore many of the issues around the area of social entrepreneurship. This next section looks at the practicalities of how to set up a social enterprise, and explores why location and social mission are so important. In addition, it looks at how to finance such an initiative.

We believe that case studies bring to life the realities of working in this area. Many social enterprises are very successful and, like other businesses, have to grapple with issues of cost and finance, and, if successful, make decisions on how and where to expand. We have selected four very different and interesting case studies. Each has a common theme, in that they all start in a particular place, each one set up in response to a need/opportunity in a particular community. In addition each one has to grapple with how to manage change and respond to developing markets. The UK case study shows that for an organisation to survive it needs to be based on a firm financial model; having commitment and a social mission is not enough. The study from the US looks at the importance of innovation within an entrepreneurial culture and the need to respond to a changing environment. The study from India shows that social enterprises can be influenced and affected by global markets. The final case study of a social enterprise from China differs from the others in that its very survival is totally dependent on its ability to trade, whereas the other three have obtained grant funding to either part fund their project or support new developments.

These four very different case studies enable the reader to apply the understanding from previous chapters to related case examples. Although each organisation can be 'badged' under a broad label of social enterprises each one is unique, responding to local need within a very distinct cultural environment. We believe that understanding this clear message helps the reader to understand there is not just one type of social entrepreneur and therefore not just one type of social enterprise.

The case study in Chapter Ten describes a project, Adrenaline Alley, a social enterprise that has grown out of an interest in urban sports. Mandy Young describes how and why she became a social entrepreneur, how she identified a particular need in her home area and developed an idea for a project into a viable social enterprise that offers community facilities for young people to pursue urban sports and other activities. Her personal reflection of the process adds depth to the theoretical stance taken earlier in the book, and has proved to be a very important aspect of the learning that has taken place in the teaching of social entrepreneurship.

In Chapter Eleven, Kimberly Sugden and Anthony Mendes contextualise social entrepreneurship in the US and then provide a case example, The Enterprising Kitchen, to bring this description to life. In particular, this project highlights the rapid change that organisations may experience and the role of the innovative social entrepreneur in keeping the organisation viable and on track. Although the US policy context shows clear differences to the situation in the UK, this chapter helps the reader understand what these differences are and also highlights the common experiences and skills that underpin them both.

In Chapter Twelve, Marie Tze Kwan So describes how she and her partner Carol Chyau took models developed in a US business setting and applied these when developing social enterprises in China. The reader will be able to appreciate the similarities and also differences in approach that are required in adapting ideas that have been developed in the west to different locations. This case also highlights the fact that cultural homogeneity should not be assumed and that the diversity of local people's experience should be an integral aspect of the development of specific social enterprises. Marketing local products globally to improve the lives of particular groups of people is an example of globalisation in action and illustrates how the flow of ideas and services can travel around the world. This case example relies solely on income generation rather than on a combination of income and contributions from other sources like charitable grants, in contrast to the other studies.

In Chapter Thirteen, Stan Thekaekara describes and reflects on how his political views have shaped the organisations he initiated and how his views have changed to reflect the wider evolution of global politics and the role of the market. He provides details of the organisation Just Change and the impact it has had, not just in India, but also across the world by being able to link oppressed people to help them forge new solutions for tackling long-standing problems of poverty and a lack of social justice. This case study in particular shows how entrepreneurial thinking evolves over time and shapes itself to new political contexts.

In the final chapter, we summarise the benefits to be gained from applying a skills approach to understanding social entrepreneurship. We do this by identifying what is needed to analyse, instigate, sustain and reflect on its different aspects and stress the links between theoretical understanding and social action in a sustainable model of delivery.

Part One
Skills in policy analysis

TWO

The place of social enterprise in UK contemporary policy

Ian Buchanan

Introduction: history and context

Social enterprise is not new to Britain. In the nineteenth century philanthropy or charity coupled with voluntary action was an important part of the social, political and religious fabric. For much of the 20th century it was misleadingly regarded simply as a stage in the development of a modern welfare state. This is an oversimplification, although it is true that many welfare functions that have been taken on by the state were met first through the actions of social entrepreneurs and voluntary activity. The National Society for the Prevention of Cruelty to Children (NSPCC) was founded in 1884 and became the most important of a number of child welfare organisations that emerged at that time to combat what has come to be known as child abuse (Prochaska, 1988). Over the years NSPCC has had a complex relationship with the growing state but it has never been replaced by the state. Its importance lies in its continuing but changing range of services and influence rather than its anticipation of state intervention.

Voluntary and state activities have developed together. In the 1960s a range of organisations emerged in response to perceived failures in state welfare provision, including Shelter in 1966 (see www.shelter.org.uk/) and Child Poverty Action Group in 1965 (see www.cpag.org.uk/). This era marked the realisation that the British welfare state could not and should not attempt to meet every welfare need through government agencies, a realisation that subsequently resulted in a proliferation of interest groups, alternative, self help and complementary services. The division of labour was in the main locally determined and there were, as there are now, significant local and regional differences in the size and capacity of the third sector (Brenton, 1985).

Social enterprises and social entrepreneurship have developed as distinctive features in the 21st century third sector. They play a significant part in contemporary UK government policy ranging from economic and social regeneration to more traditional welfare provision. Welfare voluntarism has always been influenced and regulated by government but since the late 1980s it has been transformed and joined by newer social enterprises to meet policy objectives that often blur distinctions previously made between welfare, community life, health and the economy. The larger more expansive role that social enterprises have is a product of 'marketisation' – recourse to markets as opposed to direct state provision and grant aid or charitable funding in the reconfiguration of the post-war welfare state and to their specific value and place in policy formulation (Spear, 2001).

Marketisation created the conditions for third sector development. Social enterprises and other not-for-profit organisations have also played a part in policy formulation, the effects of which are apparent in regulation and a role for not-for-profit organisations. It is argued here that despite their contribution to policy, engaging with the market has had most influence on recent development of not-for-profit organisations.

This chapter now explores:

- the parameters of third sector activity;
- the influence of policy on social enterprises (governance and regulation and community development);
- how markets influence the development of social enterprises;
- the policy context on the future and sustainability of social enterprises.

Parameters of third sector activity and social enterprises

The third sector is synonymous with social purposes. The first two sectors are the state (government) and the market (private enterprise market production). Production for social purposes differentiates social enterprises from directly delivered public services and private enterprises. That is not to say that the state and private enterprise do not have social purposes. The distinction is that the third sector is exclusively concerned with social purposes (Bridge et al, 2009).

The third sector is a generic term for organisations or associations that are part of civil society, neither within the direct control of government nor solely products of the market economy. Civil society comprises individual citizens acting collectively and autonomously to meet social purposes. This definition encompasses organisations as varied as sports clubs, community groups, national charities and trades unions.

The influence of policy on social enterprises

In relation to the provision of welfare, volunteering has always been an important part of the third sector. An example of this is the system of charitable trustees who give their time voluntarily to manage organisations. However, paid employment has always had a place alongside volunteering in the traditional third sector (for example, professional staff in the NSPCC). New social enterprises tend to employ staff but some also engage with volunteers or unpaid trainees.

Changes in governance have tended to reduce the influence of voluntarism in the sector. There has been a shift from governance by trust boards (regulated by charity law) to company boards as many organisations have chosen to become companies limited by guarantee (regulated by company law) (Spear, 2001). Recourse to company law provides protection from the risks associated with individual financial liability, in the event of the organisation becoming insolvent, and civil liability (being sued for damages by service users).

Criticism of the failings of direct state service provision (statism) came from both the political right and left before the reconfiguration of the welfare state began (Klein, 1993). Although marketisation, a favoured policy option of the rising new right in the 1980s was largely triumphant, social ideas that underpin the third sector have also been influential in debates and continue to help shape policy. With its social purposes the third sector is associated with concepts that are important to civil society like community, citizenship and collectivity. The career of Michael Young exemplifies putting these community development concepts into action (Briggs, 2001). Young went from co-authoring famous studies of post-war community life (Willmott and Young, 1960; Young and Willmott, 1980), to help found the Consumers Association (the champion of the individual consumer) and the Institute of Community Studies (devoted to community action and latterly to the idea of social entrepreneurship), which merged with the Mutual Aid Society in 2005 to form the Michael Young Foundation (see www.youngfoundation.org.uk).

The dominant political influence on the development of the third sector in Britain in the early 21st century has been *New Labour* which has drawn on the tradition of community development and associated action aimed at inclusive individual and community empowerment (Mandelson, 1997; Social Exclusion Unit, 1998). Coming from Britain's socialist party this has involved little difference in principle between right and left, although it is a distinct approach. It has drawn the third sector in as a partner along with the private sector using market mechanisms (competitive contracting) associated previously with Britain's new right. The approach has stimulated new social enterprises and social entrepreneurship. The Deakin Commission into the voluntary sector (NCVO, 1995) resulted in the introduction of voluntary sector compacts and the establishment of better infrastructure (advice and development) support for contracting and market activity. The UK Prime Minister at the time of writing, Gordon Brown, was influential in shaping third sector policy from his previous position of Chancellor of the Exchequer (finance minister) (Brown, 2004). The Treasury (department of finance), which traditionally has not been involved in operational policy, was a significant source of policy ideas and publications in this area (HM Treasury, 2002).

A more expansive policy role for The Treasury can be explained in part by the content of the policy as well as by Gordon Brown's personal commitment. The Treasury is concerned with the performance of the economy and within New Labour's policy of inclusion; empowerment came to involve deprived communities taking responsibility for their own revival (Brown, 2004). Although it is not an exclusively UK phenomenon, economic renewal and individual and community empowerment were brought together to play a central role in policy. The way the policy was implemented and its market orientation was not exempt from criticism.

Amin (2005), for example, points out that it is surprising that so much should be asked of economically deprived communities but does not dismiss the idea itself in arguing for ways of working that give people greater control and autonomy.

The nature of Brown's personal commitment is best understood through his affinity with a famous fellow Scot from the same home town, Kirkaldy: Adam Smith. Brown subscribes to the reinterpretation of Smith's intellectual work that draws on *The theory of moral sentiments* to identify Smith with community values and with individual moral responsibilities to fellow citizens (see McLean, 2006). Brown's attempt to square markets and global competition with social goals is grounded in the tradition of Smith's contribution to the Scottish Enlightenment.

New Labour's policy might have developed differently had more radical elements from Michael Young come to the fore. Government policy has resulted in the exclusive use of competitive tendering processes to select suppliers of services but could have used different ways of producing services, that is, alternative modes of production. Such an alternative approach would not have implied a return to state monopoly provision. Advocates of developing approaches to producing services that align needs with empowerment include Hirst (1994), a promoter of modern cooperation and democratic participation. Hirst, a founding signatory of Charter 88, the democratic reform organisation, argues for 'associative democracy' to produce more involvement in social and economic action based on social principles and associationism. Working in this way would give preference to cooperative production, user-controlled organisations and community enterprises for social production. Enterprises of this kind exist but they do not constitute a preferred mode of production or the dominant approach to social provision.

Defining community participation in this way has a shared lineage with Michael Young's activities through the promotion of the third enlightenment value, fraternity (community orientation). An important element of this approach is that empowerment and participation require engagement beyond the market and being a consumer. This contrasts with the basis for competitive tendering that is made in relation to people using social care services through the entirely reasonable sounding statement that people who use services do not care who provides them, only that they meet their needs. It is, however, difficult to square such a value free statement with individual and community empowerment and autonomy and control.

Market influence on the development of social enterprises

Markets have influenced the development of social enterprises through changed funding arrangements. In the 19th and first half of the 20th centuries voluntary organisations funded their pressure group activities, innovations and services by raising funds directly from the public by donations or through large gifts. After the advent of the welfare state they continued to fulfil these roles, increasingly relying on local or national government grants, including those from the National Health Service (NHS). The share of sources of income varied enormously in different voluntary organisations, however, before marketisation government funding increased to become the greater share of voluntary resources. There was a consequent fear that reliance on the state might tend to undermine the independence and autonomy that are central to voluntarism. Marketisation changed the method of allocating funding from grants (with a presumption of continuity and significant discretion over provision) to issuing specific time-limited contracts through competitive tendering processes.

These changes are well illustrated if we return to the example of the NSPCC, a notably successful organisation under both grant aid and contracting. In the 19th century, as a new organisation with wide public appeal, the NSPCC was one of the most successful at raising money by donation through community collectors and the support of privileged middle-class children (Prochaska, 1988). With the advent of the welfare state it combined significant fund raising with government and local authority grant aid and has subsequently adapted well to contract culture. Although it has retained very significant fund raising capacity (for example through its 'Full Stop' campaign to combat child abuse, gift and other product sales), central and local government contracts have tied the organisation closely to national child care policy. The NSPCC has, however, retained sufficient independence to have influence on the shape of national child care policy's development and implementation (see www.nspcc.org.uk/). The same may not be true of large organisations with limited independent funds, smaller voluntary organisations or new social enterprises. In their case they may be forced to respond to policy changes in order to ensure continued funding rather than help shape them, notwithstanding their participation in consultations and in local implementation and planning through Local Strategic Partnerships (LSPs).

Marketisation allied to Britain's powerful central government has shaped the third sector. Central government is no longer neutral with the passing of the system that saw the role of central government largely in terms of providing a legislative framework and accompanying regulation. These set the parameters for services while leaving responsibility for implementation and development largely to the local state (local government and local NHS administration) (Day and Klein, 1987). The public sector management revolution with its focus on performance measured through goals and targets sets a framework which provides opportunities for third sector social enterprises (Pollitt, 2003). The transformation of these arrangements and the extension of central government power are best understood through a brief case study of the introduction and development of Community Care Reform in the 1990s.

The latest community care policy reformulation in Britain followed a review, *Community care agenda for change* (Griffiths, 1988), a White Paper, *Community care: The next 10 years and beyond* (Department of Health, 1989) and new legislation, the 1990 National Health Service and Community Care Act. There were many facets to the reforms but for the current purposes two were particularly significant: the introduction of care management and the creation of a mixed economy of care. These were aimed at extending choice, matching the assessed needs of recipients of community care support and services. Choice was to be increased without turning them into direct consumers, spending money in the marketplace. Instead a system of quasi markets, that gave impetus to marketisation, was formed.

The introduction of care management resulted in care managers being promoted as a way of ensuring that older people, people with disabilities, people with mental health problems and others who need support and care paid for from public funds can exercise choice over who provides that care and the form that it takes. This marked the introduction of a consumerist approach in the adult social care system.

The promotion of a mixed economy of care signalled the end of the dominance of directly provided services. The policy laid emphasis on the provision of high-quality services from the public and independent (private and voluntary) sectors.

The reforms created quasi-markets in social care. A quasi-market is one which simulates market mechanisms, by providing consumer choice by introducing competition. It is not a traditional market, however, because the individual service user does not buy the service therefore there is no consumer sovereignty (Glennerster and Le Grand, 1994). Services are purchased by care managers (micro-purchasers) and service commissioners (macro-purchasers). The latter set up purchase contracts of varied type. Block contracts take up a fixed amount of a service whether it is fully used or not. Other contracts call off a service from a tendered list at an agreed price and sometimes with a guaranteed minimum take-up. They also use spot purchases where there is no price agreement between the supplier and the commissioner (Means et al, 2008).

The system of care management is based on assessment of individual need, which is the basis for managing the market by commissioners. Griffiths (1988) placed great emphasis on individual choice but was not confident that the conventional consumer marketplace could satisfy the complex and changing needs of community care service users. The care management system has been associated with significant innovation and flexibility in meeting community care needs and this has provided opportunities for the third sector (and the private sector). Nevertheless, it has come under consistent and sometimes severe criticism (Glendinning and Means, 2006). In practice service users' needs are very diverse. Some are significant but predictable and can be met relatively easily; others are complex and changing. The pressure for flexibility in quasi-markets, including recent proposals to introduce reforms that approximate more closely to markets through the introduction of individual budgets for people using services (Glendinning and Means, 2006), poses challenges for enterprises and the sustainability of third sector organisations. The critique that follows is widely applicable beyond community care.

The future and sustainability of social enterprises

Quasi-markets have led to out-sourcing or privatisation in many parts of the UK government system. As well as providing opportunities for social enterprises and social entrepreneurs this creates vulnerability to fluctuations in economic activity and government spending. Out-sourced services tend to be considered as marginal in comparison to those that remain in house. If previous experience is repeated cuts in public spending are made where reductions can be achieved quickly, particularly where this can be done without stopping services completely. Domiciliary community care and youth work fall into this category, although with the extensive use of tendering all services are vulnerable to adjustments in volume and service specifications. The way in which contracting works in the third sector reinforces this vulnerability and leads to a number of challenges to the sustainability of social enterprises.

Instability in the economics of social enterprises

Instability derives from the way contracting has worked in the third sector. Third sector funding through contracts does not cover the full or sustainable costs of provision. In part this is a hangover from the voluntary sector grant aid system that supplemented organisations' fund raising in pursuit of what were seen as shared social purposes in the shape of services developed by voluntary organisations. Within the system of contracting, which is by definition led by the organisation letting the contract, this approach has been modified to a form of 'leverage' or matched funding, where, for example, a local authority with a limited budget will maximise its purchasing power through contracting. This is achieved by paying only part of the costs of a service or by making the contract time limited. The money spent by the local authority attracts extra resources in pursuit of the contractor's goals. The service provider is expected to find the shortfall in the funding or the continuation funding through a variety of means (including market activity, finding partnership or matching funders, and targeted fund raising).

It is referred to as leverage because funding is used as an incentive to attract or lever more funds into the service from other sources, a process which has accelerated the growth and development of social enterprises and voluntary organisations. It is promoted as partnership working and joining up organisations in which the element of shared social purpose, usually instigated by the third sector, is replaced by specified activity that meets the general good as determined by government and government agencies. However, in maximising growth it introduces an element of instability. Leverage leaves third sector organisations vulnerable to loss of funding. Leverage can work in reverse, so that in the same way as it enhances growth by maximising income it can also accelerate decline when funding streams are interrupted or stop growing. This could be through cuts in public spending or, given its importance, changes in lottery funding policy.

Confusion about 'the place' of value-based organisations

Social enterprises are valued by government and citizens for being of the community and for their social purposes. When the government introduced the policy of *Best Value* in 1998 as the successor to compulsory competitive tendering (CCT) it created the possibility that a distinct social and economic place for the third sector might be created. Best Value was sharply distinguished from the 'contract culture' associated with CCT (Vincent-Jones, 1999). However, it is value neutral and associated with the prevalent view that if the service user is satisfied then it does not matter where the service comes from. Best Value does not recognise or give preference to any particular mode of supply, but social enterprises have an advantage as vehicles that can meet the emancipatory expectations that many service users quite rightly have. Despite the intensions ascribed to Best Value in relation to CCT it has developed into a process characterised by tendering and contracting once purchasing patterns are set. This intensifies the tension between the importance of the market in the recent development of the third sector and its value base. Government has, for example, found it desirable to identify the need for a user-controlled service in adult social care in every part of the country to promote the service user voice. Under current commissioning regimes this singular requirement is unlikely to satisfy the call for emancipatory services, and in areas where there are already a number of such services the existence of some may perversely be threatened in commissioning plans based on targets.

The 'equal treatment approach' and the questions over incentives to social enterprise

Social justice secured through competitive tendering as a means of being fair to potential service suppliers is routinely referred to as a goal by service commissioners. It is argued that it is unfair to let a contract without a competitive tender because there may be a worthy organisation that could do the job better than an existing supplier. The implication is that tendering does more than secure efficiency and effectiveness but competition as social justice or an 'equal treatment approach' ignores the need to create a climate which supports social entrepreneurship.

The view that tendering and contracting amount to a just process is understandable given its basis in contract law. However, it overlooks the impact on fairness of resource differences between competing organisations and, more importantly, it overlooks the need to protect and foster social innovations. Larger organisations with bid writing expertise, marketing resources and the resources to survive periods of funding shortage are clearly at an advantage. Disadvantages to smaller, usually local, organisations have been partly addressed by voluntary sector infrastructure support but remain real (HM Treasury, 2002; OPM and Compass Partnership, 2004; see also www.thecompact.org.uk).

In practice social entrepreneurs do not receive or expect to receive protection for their socially beneficial innovations. They are usually happy to see them copied and introduced generally where they are transferable. Some names are copyright but branding has not prevented the dissemination of social processes themselves. However, this does not exempt social innovation from the general argument that it is necessary to create a climate and structure which will promote entrepreneurship and innovation. Having recourse to tendering to continue services which have been developed by social entrepreneurs is likely to have implications for entrepreneurship. The most important is to discourage the social entrepreneur in particular, and possibly social entrepreneurs in general, from developing their ideas in future. In such a situation the marketplace is cold and depersonalised and antagonistic to the values that make them work to develop socially valued services. Alienation of this kind is particularly likely where the tender is lost to either an organisation from outside the area or where the service is taken over by a private for-profit organisation. These are circumstances which raise questions about the sustainability of value based innovations that draw heavily on local effort and networks when they are put out to tender.

Dominance of public policy over the third sector

A final challenge to social enterprises comes from the dominance of public policy over the third sector. Mention of the tendency to shift from shared social purposes located outside government to the general good as determined by commissioners has already been made. The particular circumstances that have brought this control about are the New Labour government's fostering of an integrated approach to priority setting across sectors. This was made possible through agreements, notably the compact with the voluntary sector (see www.thecompact.org.uk) and the introduction of local strategic partnerships to set and monitor initiatives. The resulting structure is highly directive.

Voluntary and not-for-profit organisations receive infrastructure support designed to help them thrive in a much changed world. At one level government policy brought much needed change. It is intended to promote cohesion and to limit duplication to make it possible to tackle social issues, about which there is a consensus, successfully. However, there are drawbacks related to the nature and extent of the entanglement of government and civil society. The replacement of grant aid with contracting allied to managerialist targets has brought cohesion by imposing greater controls over the third sector. Added to this the partnership structures that have been created tend to blur the distinction between public money and philanthropic money. This may result in better services but it transforms the distinction between government and civil society beyond the need for regulation by introducing partnership that is arguably led by government, rather than by citizens. Government priorities influence all social funders so that government, philanthropic and lottery funding broadly mirror each other. Government's intention is to build a social consensus rather than dictate priorities but the tendency to be initiative driven has the effect of continuously reordering priorities. For example, in the years after the 2001 Learning Disability White Paper in England, *Valuing people*, adults with learning difficulties were a high priority for many funders. They remain a priority but a lesser priority. Changing priorities may well be healthy but it tends to create problems with sustainability because of the funder consensus that it implies.

Conclusion

The third sector is defined by its ability to adapt to change. In the UK it has expanded since the 1980s in response to the stimulus given by market approaches. This has challenged its value base and brought new vulnerabilities to market forces. Government-driven marketisation has also blurred the traditional distinction separating social enterprises in civil society from the state. This chapter has raised important questions about the sustainability of change because of economic insecurity, competition, the loss of a distinct place for the third sector and the sector's control through government policy. In identifying challenges to social enterprise it is important to acknowledge the resilience of such activity and its history of accommodation with the state and influence on it. It would be premature to argue that citizen-led social purposes have been irretrievably lost or that the sector faces economic calamity. What marks the third sector out is its resilience and flexibility.

This resilience will be tested in the next few years in the UK because of the financial crisis that has affected western economies. However, what has become apparent in many neo-liberal economies and also in Scandinavian countries is a desire to look to the third sector to provide innovative solutions for social problems. As the European Commission President José Manuel Barroso said: 'The financial and economic crisis makes creativity and innovation in general and social innovation in particular even more important to foster sustainable growth, secure jobs and boost competitiveness' (Europa, 2009). The question is then whether social enterprises are able to fulfil this role.

References

Amin, A. (2005) 'Local community on trial', *Economy and Society*, vol 34, no 4, pp 612-33.

Brenton, M. (1985) *The voluntary sector in British social services*, Harlow: Longman.

Bridge, S., Murtagh, B. and O'Neill, K. (2009) *Understanding the social economy and third sector*, Basingstoke: Palgrave.

Briggs, A. (2001) *Michael Young, social entrepreneur*, Basingstoke: Palgrave.

Brown, G. (2004) Keynote address to the NCVO Annual Conference, 2004 (www. ncvo-vol.org.uk/search/node/gordon brown keynote address).

Day, P. and Klein, R. (1987) *Accountabilities: Five public services*, London: Tavistock.

Department of Health (1989) *Caring for people. Community care in the next decade and beyond*, Cm 849, London: HMSO.

Europa (2009) 'President Barroso discusses how to boost "social innovation"', Europa Press Release Ref IP/09/81 (http://europa.eu/rapid/pressReleasesAction.do?reference=IP/09/81&format=HTML&aged).

Glendinning, C. and Means, R. (2006) 'Personal social services: developments in adult social care', in L. Bauld, K. Clarke, and T. Maltby (eds), *Social Policy Review 18*, Bristol: The Policy Press/Social Policy Association.

Glennerster, H. and Le Grand, J. (1994) *The development of quasi-markets in welfare provision*, (WSP/102), London: London School of Economics.

Griffiths, Sir R. (1988) *Community care agenda for action: Report to the Secretary of State for the Social Services*, London: HMSO.

Hirst, P. (1994) *Associative democracy: New forms of economic and social governance*, Cambridge: Polity Press.

HM Treasury (2002) *The role of the voluntary and community sector in service delivery*, London: The Stationery Office.

Klein, R. (1993) 'O'Goffe's tale', in C. Jones (ed) *New perspectives on the welfare state in Europe*, London: Routledge.

McLean, I. (2006) *Adam Smith, radical and egalitarian: An interpretation for the 21st century*, Edinburgh: Edinburgh University Press.

Mandelson, P. (1997) *Labour's next steps: Tackling social exclusion*, Fabian Pamphlet no 581, London: Fabian Society.

Means, R., Richards, S. and Smith, R. (2008) *Community care: Policy and practice*, Basingstoke: Palgrave.

NCVO (National Council for Voluntary Organisations) (1995) *Commission on the Future of the Voluntary Sector: Meeting the challenge of change: Voluntary action in the 21st century*, Chaired by Professor Nicholas Deakin, London: NCVO.

OPM and Compass Partnership (2004) *Voluntary and community sector infrastructure: Final report*, Prepared on behalf of the Active Communities Unit, London: OPM Compass.

Pollitt, C. (2003) *The essential public manager*, Maidenhead: Open University Press.

Prochaska, F. (1988) *The voluntary impulse: Philanthropy in modern Britain*, London: Faber and Faber.

Social Exclusion Unit (1998) *Bringing Britain together: a national strategy for neighbourhood renewal*, Cm 4045, London: The Stationery Office.

Spear, R. (2001) 'United Kingdom: a wide range of social enterprises', in C. Borzaga and J. Defourney (eds) *The emergence of social enterprise*, Abingdon: Routledge.

Vincent-Jones, P. (1999) 'Competition and contracting in the transition from CCT to Best Value: towards a more reflective regulation?', *Public Administration*, vol 77, no 2, pp 273-91).

Willmott, P. and Young, M. (1960) *Family and class in a London suburb*, London: Routledge and Kegan Paul.

Young, M. and Willmott, P. (1957) *Family and kinship in East London*, London: Routledge and Kegan Paul.

Website resources

Child Poverty Action Group: www.cpag.org.uk/
National Council for Voluntary Organisations: www.ncvo-vol.org.uk/
National Society for the Prevention of Cruelty to Children: www.nspcc.org.uk/
Shelter UK: shelter.org.uk/
The Compact: www.thecompact.org.uk/
The Young Foundation: www.youngfoundation.org.uk/

THREE

What do we mean by 'social enterprise'? Defining social entrepreneurship

Gladius Kulothungan

Introduction

In a previous chapter we have seen that although social enterprises have been around for over a century in their current form it is a concept that has only been popular during the last two decades. Equally, the notion of the social entrepreneur is a concept that has attracted interest from a range of people, including policy-makers and academics. A survey of social enterprises across the UK (IFF Research Ltd, 2005) identified a national population of social enterprises at around 15,000. The Annual Small Business Survey (Williams and Cowling, 2007), however, revealed that there are in fact a higher number of firms that fall into the category of social enterprises; this helped recalibrate our understanding of the total population of social enterprises, suggesting a larger population of at least 55,000 of them across the UK with a turnover of £27 billion.

This chapter will address the following questions:

- What are these social enterprises?
- What do they do and how do we understand them?
- What do we mean by social entrepreneurship?
- Why is there so much interest in social enterprises now?

The backdrop of capitalism

We live in a capitalist society where the emphasis has been on 'economic output'. Capitalism is characterised by the presence of the free market, where goods and services are produced and distributed through market mechanisms, and the state, which oversees the markets and takes responsibility for some basic service delivery using tax revenues. There is also a civil society, which consists of organisations and groupings that are distinct from government or the private sector and which complements the other two sectors with its own services to meet some unmet social needs – the third or voluntary and community sector.

One of the distinctive features of capitalist economies is that they place an emphasis on 'entrepreneurship', the ability to recognise an opportunity, innovate and create new goods or services to exploit that opportunity and bring those goods and services to the marketplace and create financial profit and return for investors. Entrepreneurship has been the driving force of capitalist economic growth for over two hundred years and the majority of 'successful' ventures in western societies have been underpinned by it. Being entrepreneurial and getting things done in innovative ways is seen as one of the most important ingredients for organisations to succeed in modern society. The UK government, for instance, places considerable emphasis on the development of 'enterprise skills' funding initiatives in secondary, further and higher education (Hussain and Matlay, 2007).

French economists used the term 'entrepreneur' as early as the 17th century, and by the 19th century Jean Baptiste Say was using the word *entrepreneur* to describe individuals who were venturesome and stimulated economic progress. According to Say, they were doing this by finding new and better ways of doing things. The idea that entrepreneurs 'create value' had become well established by the end of the 19th century. Joseph Schumpeter developed this further by introducing the concept of 'innovation' in the 20th century and focused on how entrepreneurs innovate and drive change in the economy by serving new markets or creating new ways of doing things. The emergence of the term 'Social Enterprise' and its growing popularity in the last 20 years has to be seen in this context (Dees, 2001, p 1).

Why social enterprises?

There are a few contributing factors that have led to the emergence of the concept and practice of social enterprise in recent times:

- Provision of services by the state has declined gradually from the late 1970s, with the introduction of private sector management methods into welfare provision in the late 1970s, leaving gaps in services that needed to be filled. Catford (1998), for instance, eloquently articulates the situation and the possible solution:

  Traditional welfare-state approaches are in decline globally, and in response new ways of creating healthy and sustainable communities are required. This challenges our social, economic and political systems to respond with new, creative and effective environments that support and reward change. From the evidence available, current examples of social entrepreneurship offer exciting new ways of realizing the potential of individuals and communities ... into the 21st century. (Catford, 1998 p 97)

- Market mechanisms have failed to meet the needs of people in comprehensive terms. One of the explanations for the existence of social purpose organisations is that when commercial market forces do not meet social needs sufficiently civil society organisations come in to address unmet needs. A good example of this occurred in the late 19th century with the setting up of national charities like the National Society for the Prevention of Cruelty to Children.
- There has been a rise of an 'enterprise culture', with an emphasis on self-reliance and personal responsibility in the last few decades. Coupled with this has been the emergence of a certain 'professionalism' (Bull, 2008), which has spread into public and third sector organisations.
- Funding opportunities for third sector organisations – community groups, voluntary and the not-for-profit organisations – have started moving from grant giving to contract/competitive tendering and the need to work out market-based revenue streams (Bull, 2008). There has, therefore, been a push for the third sector organisations to become more 'entrepreneurial' and move in the direction of blending values and adapting business principles to address social missions (Bull, 2008).

Situating social enterprises

Social enterprises are seen as playing a unique role in society as they are better able to respond to perceived need in more efficient ways than public agencies, private sector organisations or traditional voluntary sector organisations (Bacchiega and Borzaga, 2001).

They can be situated within the evolutionary trajectory of the 'social economy', which 'began in the nineteenth century and incorporated organisations such as co-operatives, mutual benefit societies and associations' (Laville and Nyssens, 2001, p 312). This spectrum of organisations that are, from an international perspective, part of the 'Third Sector' seems to have a unique set of characteristics, when compared to capitalist firms, which is that 'the material interest of capital investors is subject to limits, and in which creating a common patrimony is given priority over a return on individual investment' (Laville and Nyssens, 2001, p 315).

This model takes into account three key organisational worlds in modern societies: one rooted in voluntary association, the second deriving from commercial market trading, and a third rooted in public service. These three worlds each have their own distinct culture and definite set of rules for workplace organisation. The governance practices and value commitments of these three worlds are also different from each other. They can and do overlap, with the result that hybrid organisational forms develop to serve multiple interests. As this model suggests, social enterprises fill several gaps left by all three organisational worlds.

Social entrepreneurship essentially creates a hybrid organisation, with the ability of the individual entrepreneur to cross or mix a plurality of action principles with a plurality of economic principles. These principles form the foundations of social enterprises: a collective ownership, collective governance and an explicit purpose to produce positive effects on social outcomes through economic activity.

Defining social enterprises

Social enterprise seems to mean different things to different people and its definition and interpretation varies across the globe. In the US the term social enterprise is closely associated with an entrepreneurial culture, where the focus is on the individual entrepreneur far more than the collective or community (Chell, 2007). In this kind of approach the whole discussion and focus on social entrepreneurship is similar to trying to understand and promote business entrepreneurship. For example, the US case study in this volume explores some of these issues and discusses how all entrepreneurs are risk takers, but stresses the fact that they are not reckless people but those that make decisions on calculated risk. This characteristic is shown clearly in the China case study in this volume, where the two social entrepreneurs spent a great deal of time planning and identifying both product and potential markets before making their investment.

In parts of Europe, the term 'social enterprise' is characterised by its community objectives and stakeholder democracy, where the control of the organisations rests with the collective. L'Emergence des enterprises sociales en Europe (EMES) define social enterprises as autonomous organisations that benefit the community with group objectives, shared aims and a decision-making power that is not based on capital ownership (Bull, 2008). According to Hulgard and Spear (2006), however, in the UK the concept of social enterprise embraces ideas from both Europe and the US.

A Department of Trade and Industry (DTI) report, for instance, states:

> A social enterprise is a business with primarily social objectives whose surpluses are principally reinvested for that purpose in the business or in the community, rather than being driven by the need to maximise profit for shareholders and owners. (DTI, 2002, p 7)

The DTI definition underlines the primary intention of social enterprises as social organisations, clearly distinguishing them as not operating for private profit. There is also a clear focus on the enterprise as a trading business generating a surplus, thus differentiating social enterprise activity from other organisations in the charity sector, so:

> A social enterprise is not defined by its legal status but by its nature: its social aims and outcomes; the basis on which its social mission is embedded in its structure and governance; and the way it uses the profits it generates through trading activities. (New Economics Foundation/Shorebank Advisory Services, 2004, p 8)

Broad and narrow definitions

In his essay 'The meaning of "social entrepreneurship"', Dees observes:

> Though the concept of 'social entrepreneurship' is gaining popularity, it means different things to different people. This can be confusing. Many associate social entrepreneurship exclusively with not-for-profit organizations starting for-profit or earned-income ventures. Others use it to describe anyone who starts a not-for-profit organization. Still others use it to refer to business owners who integrate social responsibility into their operations. What does 'social entrepreneurship' really mean? What does it take to be a social entrepreneur? (Dees, 2001, p 1)

As we have already noted, definitions of social entrepreneurship have ranged from broad to narrow. In the broader sense social entrepreneurship refers to 'innovative value creating activity with a social objective' (Hulgard, 2008) in either the for-profit or non-profit sector. This can be in social-purpose commercial ventures, for example Fairtrade, or in corporate social entrepreneurship, which is best exemplified by the drug company Merck giving away the drug Mectizan free for millions of people affected by river blindness in Africa (Merck Report, 2008). It can also be in the non-profit sector, or across sectors, such as hybrid structural forms that mix for-profit and non-profit approaches – for example trading arms of charities like charity shops.

The narrow definition positions social entrepreneurship as the phenomenon of 'applying business expertise and market-based skills in the non-profit sector' (Wei-Skillern et al, 2007) typically when non-profit organisations develop innovative approaches to generate revenue streams and earn income. What is common across all definitions of social entrepreneurship is the stipulation that the major underlying drive for social entrepreneurship is:

> The creation of a social value that is produced in collaboration with people and organizations from the civil society who are engaged in social innovations that usually implies an economic activity. (Hulgard, 2008, p 4)

Defourny and Nyssens (2008) explicate the 'double bottom-line' imperative of social enterprises in the following way:

Criteria reflecting the economic-entrepreneurial dimension of social enterprises are:

- a continuous activity producing goods and/or selling services;
- a high degree of autonomy;
- a significant level of economic risk;
- a minimum amount of paid work.

Indicators encapsulating the social dimensions are:

- an explicit aim to benefit the community;
- an initiative launched by a group of citizens;
- a decision-making power not based on capital ownership;
- a participatory nature, which involves various parties affected by the activity;
- a limited profit distribution.

Recognising opportunities

Research on social entrepreneurship has consistently acknowledged opportunity recognition as a vital feature of social entrepreneurs. Seelos and Mair (2005) state that social entrepreneurs recognise and act on opportunities to improve systems, create solutions and invent new approaches to tackling social problems.

Thompson (2002) adapted Sykes' three-stage entrepreneurial process into a four stage process composed of the following steps:

- envisioning – perceiving an opportunity;
- engaging – engaging the opportunity with a mind to do something about it;
- enabling – ensuring something happens by acquiring the necessary resources;
- enacting – championing and leading the project.

Dees (1998) makes the case that social entrepreneurs see opportunity where others see problems. He defines social entrepreneurs as people who:

- adopt a mission to create and sustain social value;
- recognise and relentlessly pursue new opportunities to serve that mission
- engage in a process of continuous innovation, adaptation and learning;
- act boldly without being limited by resources currently in hand;
- exhibit heightened accountability to the constituents served and for the outcomes created.

Social entrepreneurs are 'energetic, persistent, and unusually confident, with an ability to inspire others to join them in their work' (Barendsen and Gardner, 2004, p 45). They are also deeply committed to their cause, very independent, and able to explain the link between their specific goals and a broader picture of an alternative world.

The idea of social innovation

The idea of innovation has been a key element in understanding social enterprises. Social innovation is about developing innovative solutions to poverty alleviation or social exclusion. Mulgan (2006, p 6) defines social innovation as referring to 'new ideas that work in meeting social goals'. The definition he proposes is where social innovation is the development of innovative activities and services that are motivated by the goal of meeting a social need; and they are predominantly developed and diffused through organisations whose primary purposes are social. These can be called organisations with specific social missions. The subject of innovation is addressed further in Tim Curtis's chapter on the challenge and risks of innovation in social entrepreneurship.

Social enterprises as hybrid organisations

There have been some discussions on how social enterprises hybridise the three different poles of our economies to serve social needs. The three poles are posited as:

1. The *market economy*, where circulation of goods and services take place in a market setting;
2. The *non-market economy*, where the circulation of goods and services takes place under the auspices and jurisdiction of the welfare state, where there is a redistribution;
3. The *non-monetary economy*, where goods and services are exchanged on the basis of reciprocity (Laville and Nyssens, 2001).

It could be argued that social enterprises are a hybridised form of capitalism and that they probably represent a higher evolutionary form of capitalism.

There is an important feature that distinguishes social enterprises from capitalist firms, which is that social enterprises focus on 'the collective benefit' – benefits that accrue to the whole community in which they operate and not just for the ownership. As argued by Laville and Nyssons (2001, p 319) the 'collective benefits are not simply induced by economic activity but are, rather, a dimension claimed by those who promote and actually undertake the activity'. The very pursuit of collective benefits acts as the spur and motivation to setting up of social enterprises and the very incentive of initiating them. While in capitalist enterprises 'the positive externalities discourage the private investments by socialising the benefits' (Callon, 1999, p 14), in 'social enterprises the positive externalities are among the reasons why stakeholders join a collective action to create economic activity' (Laville and Nyssons, 2001, p 320).

Characteristics of social enterprises

Social enterprises, especially those that are situated within the third sector, are also seen as organisations that have sprung up as an ethical response to the prevalent inequalities and injustices today (Kulothungan, 2009). The ethical–institutional response of social enterprises to social injustice and inequality can be seen in the following propositions:

- **Proposition 1:** Social enterprises nurture multiple stakeholders, including whole communities.
- **Proposition 2:** Social enterprises build activities on relationship based networks – social capital and mutualities.
- **Proposition 3:** Social enterprises take care of the developmental aspects of various stakeholders in them. Process becomes more important than product.
- **Proposition 4:** Social enterprises 'keep it all in the family', by the mechanism of asset lock or no-profit distribution illustrated by community interest companies in the UK.

Emergence of social enterprises

'How do social enterprises emerge?' has been a question asked in academia but as yet has not been answered comprehensively. Scholars have suggested that personality characteristics, childhood experiences, family background and professional experiences play a role in determining who becomes a social entrepreneur (Barendsen and Gardner 2004). The motivations and aims of the social entrepreneur involved in the setting up of social enterprises have not yet been looked at rigorously. Social entrepreneurs may have significant personal credibility (for example past records of success), which they use to tap into critical resources and build the necessary network of participating organisations (Waddock and Post 1991). Social entrepreneurs draw on their past careers, contacts, and status to mobilise resources.

Conclusion

The view that social enterprises are here to stay is shown by the development of specific legal forms in some European countries. *Community interest companies* (CIC), for instance, were introduced in the UK in 2005 and *impresa sociale* in Italy in 2006 (Ridley-Duff, 2008). What is common in both is the introduction of a cross-ownership organisational form. This can be taken up by traditional cooperatives and mutual organisations; by entrepreneurial non-profit organisations; and by investor-owned firms when they respect the requirements and constraints imposed by law. Key constraints are imposed on profit distribution, while the firm is required to pursue a public benefit aim. Multi-stakeholdership is the hallmark of these forms where governance is openly democratic with the widest participation by the community, beneficiaries and other stakeholders.

References

Bacchiega, A. and Borzaga, C. (2001) 'Social enterprises as incentive structures: an economic analysis', in C. Borzaga and J. Defourney (eds) *The emergence of social enterprise*, London: Routledge, pp 273-95.

Barendsen, L. and Gardner, H. (2004) 'Is the social entrepreneur a new type of leader?', *Leader to Leader*, vol 2004, no 34, pp 43-50.

Bull, M. (2008) 'Challenging tensions: critical, theoretical and empirical perspectives on social enterprise', *International Journal of Entrepreneurial Behaviour and Research*, vol 14, no 5, pp 268-75.

Callon, M. (1999) 'Actor-network theory: the market test', in J. Law and J. Hassard (eds) *Actor network and after*, Oxford and Keele: Blackwell and *Sociological Review*, pp 181-95.

Catford, J. (1998) 'Social entrepreneurs are vital for health promotion – but they need supportive environments too', *Health Promotion International*, vol 13, no 2, pp.95-7.

Chell, E. (2007) 'Social enterprise and entrepreneurship: towards a convergent theory of the entrepreneurial process', *International Small Business Journal*, vol. 25, part 1, pp 5-26.

Dees, J.G. (2001) 'The meaning of "social entrepreneurship"', reformatted and revised 30 May (www.caseatduke.org/documents/dees_sedef.pdf).

Defourney, J. and Nyssens, M. (2008) 'Social enterprise in Europe: recent trends and developments', *Social Enterprise Journal*, vol 4, no 3, pp 202-22.

DTI (Department of Trade and Industry) (2002) *A strategy for success*, London: HM Treasury.

Hulgard, L. (2008) 'Discources of social entrepreneurship in USA and Europe – variations of the same theme?', Paper for the 8th International Conference of ISTR, Barcelona, 9-12 July.

Hulgard, L. and Spear, R. (2006) 'Social entrepreneurship and mobilisation of social capital in European social enterprises', in M. Nyssens (ed) *Social Enterprise*, London: Routledge, pp 85-108.

Hussain, J. and Matlay, H. (2007) 'Vocational education and training in small ethnic minority businesses in the UK, *Education and Training*, vol 49, no 8/9, pp 671-85.

IFF Research Ltd (2005) *A survey of social enterprises across the UK: Research report prepared for the Small Business Service* (www.cabinetoffice.gov.uk/media/cabinetoffice/third_sector/assets/survey_social_enterprise_across_uk.pdf).

Kulothungan, G (2009) 'From intention formation to intentional action: the situational logic of social enterprise formation', Paper presented at the 2nd EMES International Research Conference on Social Enterprise, Trento, Italy, 1-4 July.

Laville, J. and Nyssens, M. (2001) 'The social enterprise: towards a theoretical socio-economic approach', in C. Borzaga and J. Defourney, (eds) *The emergence of social enterprise*, London: Routledge, pp 312–32.

Merck Report (2008) *The Merck MECTIZAN® donation program: 20 years of progress* (www.merck.com/corporate-responsibility/docs/MDP-Backgrounder-2008.pdf).

Mulgan, G. (2006) *Social innovation, what it is, why it matters and how it can be accelerated*, London: The Young Foundation.

New Economics Foundation/Shorebank Advisory Services (2004) *Unlocking the potential*, London: The Social Enterprise Coalition.

Ridley-Duff, R. (2008) 'Social enterprise as a socially rational business', *International Journal of Entrepreneurial Behaviour and Research*, vol 14, no 5, pp 291-312.

Seelos, C. and Mair, J. (2005) 'Social entrepreneurship: creating new business models to serve the poor', *Business Horizons*, vol 48, pp 241-46.

Thompson, J. (2002) 'The world of the social entrepreneur', *The International Journal of Public Sector Management*, vol 15, no 5, pp 412-31.

Waddock, S. and Post, J. (1991) 'Social entrepreneurs and catalytic change', *Public Administration Review*, vol 51, no 5, pp 393-401.

Wei-Skillern, J., Austin, J., Leonard, H. and Stevenson, H. (2007) *Entrepreneurship in the Social Sector*, London: Sage.

Williams, M. and Cowling, M. (2007) *Annual Small Business Survey 2007*, Department for Business Innovation and Skills, UK (www.berr.gov.uk/files/file50124.doc).

Part Two
Skills for social entrepreneurship

FOUR

Identifying need

Richard Bryant

Introduction

> Authentic community development and enterprise emerges out of the
> needs and experiences of local people. It is a collective expression of
> human creativity, often in the face of hardship, adversity and opposition.
> (Bryant, 1989, p 4)

Identifying and responding to social need is at the heart of community
development and social enterprise. This chapter examines definitions of need,
approaches to identifying need and the skills and qualities which can facilitate
successful practice.

The focus of the chapter is on locality based community organisations and
enterprises, which operate in areas such as housing estates, villages or a cluster
of neighbourhoods. Although large national voluntary organisations tend to
command most of the political and media attention, it is important to remember
that the majority of community organisations and social enterprises in the UK
are locally based, employ few staff and are heavily dependent on volunteers (HM
Treasury and Cabinet Office, 2007).

Defining need

Defining need can be difficult and contested, as is evident from the long-standing
debates over the meaning and measurement of poverty in the UK (Flaherty
et al, 2004). Doyal and Gough (1991) argue that there are two basic universal
needs, physical health and personal autonomy, which if not fulfilled will prevent
individuals from participating in society and realising their potential as human
beings. Physical health is the need for safe housing, clothing and food and personal
autonomy is the need for individuals to have the opportunity to make decisions
and choices about their lives. With some notable exceptions, such as groups
working with the homeless and asylum seekers, community organisations in the
UK tend to focus on need which relates to personal autonomy, such as improving
facilities and services, working to create safer environments and supporting groups
to participate in civil and political action.

Bradshaw (1972) suggests that there are four main ways in which people and organisations define need: normative, felt, expressed and comparative.

Normative need

Normative definitions are what experts, policy makers and administrators define as need:

> A desirable standard is laid down and is compared with the standard that actually exists – if an individual or group falls short of the desirable standard then they are identified as being in need. (Bradshaw, 1972, p 33)

Normative definitions are an integral part of British social policy and welfare legislation. Examples include the Households Below Average Income (HBAI) standard for measuring people living on low incomes, standards relating to inequalities in health and definitions of what constitutes a 'decent home'. Over recent years normative definitions have also been increasingly used to assess the 'quality of life' of local communities, particularly in relation to levels of volunteering and citizen participation (Chanan, 2004). Although normative definitions are invariably based on considerable research and empirical data they cannot be assumed to represent 'objective' standards and measures of need. Experts may disagree over the definitions of standards, and different value perspectives on what constitutes the 'good society' can shape normative definitions. Also political expediency, particularly in relation to the availability of public resources, can influence how decisions about definitions are made.

Normative definitions have a major influence on the allocation of resources to local areas and community organisations. This can be illustrated by reference to the Indices of Multiple Deprivation (IMD), which are currently used by UK central and local government and a range of other funding bodies as key criteria for targeting resources to local areas (Office of the Deputy Prime Minister, 2004). Devised by the Social Disadvantage Research Centre at Oxford University, the IMD provides measures of multiple deprivation at a small area level. The small area level is called 'Super Output Areas' (SOA) and is based on a geography used in the 2001 Census. Each SOA has an average of 1,500 residents and is normally coterminous with local electoral boundaries.

The IMD is based on the premise that multiple deprivation is made up of separate dimensions or domains, which can be measured individually and then combined to provide a composite measure. The IMD comprises seven domains

- income deprivation
- employment deprivation
- health deprivation and disability
- education, skills and training deprivation

- barriers to housing
- crime
- living environment deprivation.

Each domain is measured by a range of statistical data, derived from the Census, central and local government records, health authorities and other sources. For instance, the income deprivation domain includes data derived from Income Support, Job Seekers Allowance, Working Tax Credit and the National Asylum Support Service. A weighted statistical score is calculated for each SOA, based on the individual domains and a total score. SOAs are ranked according to their scores, providing a measure of relative deprivation across the country. There are 32,482 SOAs in England, with 1 being ranked as the most deprived.

The IMD has been used to inform New Labour's social policies since the late 1990s, particularly in relation to regeneration programmes and other area based programmes which are designed to tackle poverty and social exclusion. For instance, the National Strategy for Neighbourhood Renewal (Neighbourhood Renewal Unit, 2001) targeted extra resources to those local authorities in England which had the poorest neighbourhoods as measured by the IMD. The IMD has some obvious implications for community organisations. Organisations which are based in local areas that score relatively high in terms of the IMD are normally better placed to receive funding and infrastructure support from the state than are groups located in areas that are ranked as being less disadvantaged.

Felt need

Felt definitions of need are at the other end of the spectrum from normative definitions. Whereas normative definitions may aspire to be objective, felt definitions are essentially based on the self assessment of need and reflect life experiences, subjective feelings and expectations. Felt need can be equated with want and this equation has, in the past, tended to make some policy makers and experts sceptical of using felt need as a measure of 'real need':

> Felt need is, by itself, an inadequate measure of 'real need'. It is limited by the perceptions of the individual – whether they know there is a service available, as well as a reluctance in many situations to confess to a loss of independence. On the other hand, it is thought to be inflated by those who ask for help without really needing it. (Bradshaw, 1972, p 33)

Felt need has always been a focus for voluntary action and many community organisations have their origins in responding to collective expressions of felt need that highlight material disadvantages and inadequate services in local areas. For instance, the early history of tenants associations and community associations in the UK provides numerous examples of groups being established in response to unmet need related to poor housing conditions and a lack of community facilities and meeting places (Milligan, 1961). A common ingredient in these and other forms of community action is that the felt need was invariably shared by large numbers of residents and was not confined to the individual wants of a few households.

Over the last four decades the significance of felt need has been increasingly recognised by statutory bodies and a wide range of other welfare organisations. This has been due to a complex interplay of factors, which include a political shift away from centralised 'top-down' approaches to the planning and delivery of services; the impact of market models of consumer choice on the public sector; demands from service users and pressure groups for more engagement in the making of social policies; and a focus on local areas and neighbourhoods as a location for tackling social disadvantage (Mayo and Robertson, 2003). As a consequence there has been a marked growth in programmes and research which are concerned with identifying and addressing the felt need of residents and local groups.

Expressed need

Expressed need is felt need translated into action and demand that is registered with the appropriate authorities and agencies. In the public sector, waiting lists for hospitals and social housing provide examples of indicators of expressed need; at the local level, community groups can act as a mouthpiece for expressing felt need in relation to a wide range of issues relating to the local environment and services. However, felt need is not always expressed and often remains hidden. Individuals and groups may be reluctant to express their needs, because of discrimination, fear of losing their independence (for example older people), lack of knowledge about the services that are available or because they have no confidence in the relevant authorities responding to their needs. Inequalities in power – especially relating to class, gender, race and age – can marginalise individuals and groups and can inhibit their voices being heard.

Community organisations have a key role to play in translating felt need into expressed need, especially in relation to those individuals and groups who are relatively powerless. Performing this role is challenging, because the individuals and groups who are marginalised tend also to be under-represented in terms of participating in community groups, and the process of providing a voice involves addressing the motivational, political and economic barriers which inhibit citizen participation and voluntary activity (Active Community Unit, 1999).

Comparative need

Comparative definitions focus on comparing the needs and circumstances of similar groups across different areas. For instance, if people with learning disabilities in one local authority area are not receiving the same level of social service support, compared with similar groups in other areas, they could be considered to be in comparative need. Comparative definitions are based on normative standards and can be used to map need relating to a range of social circumstances across the country. Examples include the IMD, the report of the Joseph Rowntree Foundation on the geographical distribution of poverty and wealth in Britain (Dorling et al, 2007) and the health profiles for local authorities and regions produced by the Association of Public Health Observatories (2008), which maps health inequalities across England according to 30 key indicators. For community organisations comparative data on need can be important in terms of compiling funding bids and raising awareness of the broader social and economic context in which local groups operate.

Identifying community need

The UK has a long history of research into the needs and social circumstances of local communities, which can be traced back to Charles Booth's pioneering studies of poverty in London in the 1880s and 1890s (Fried and Elman, 1971) and the more modest investigations of the Charity Organisation Society and the University Settlement Houses (Leat,1975). There is also a rich tradition of sociological studies of local communities in the UK, of which perhaps the best known are the studies of the East End of London carried out by the Institute of Community Studies (for example Dench et al, 2006). This literature provides invaluable insights into the changes in the social structure of local areas and the influences which shape group and family relationships and is required reading for those community development workers who are employed to help people find common cause on issues that affect them (Community Development Foundation, 2006).

There is also a long history of community groups and volunteers carrying out small-scale surveys of areas and neighbourhoods. In 1950, a handbook for community centres and associations noted that:

> One of the most worthwhile tasks which any association can carry out, is a survey of its own neighbourhood. Such surveys range from a modest attempt to assess the existing provision for recreation in order to prove the need for a community centre, to a full scale survey of all the services and amenities of the neighbourhood, with a view to meeting the needs which are revealed. (NCSS, 1950, p 59)

In the 1960s and 1970s there was a significant growth in voluntary action and the funding by the state of area-based community programmes, including the Home Office funded Community Development Project and a wide range of programmes funded under the Urban Programme. These developments were a response to a complex range of factors, which included the 'rediscovery of poverty' in the UK, concerns about race relations and conflicts in inner city areas and increases in unemployment (Popple, 1995). There was also the impact of a new wave of welfare pressure groups and social movements that focused their energy on extra-parliamentary action, including organising in local communities. One of the most ambitious of these initiatives was the Notting Hill Summer Project (NHSP), which in 1967 launched a major campaign against poor housing conditions and tenant exploitation. Influenced by the experiences of the American Civil Rights movement the NHSP involved a hundred volunteers who surveyed around 5,000 households in the area, gathering information on rents, ownership and the conditions of properties (O'Malley, 1977).

Since the 1960s and 1970s compiling information on local areas – variously described as community profiles, audits, appraisals or needs assessments – has gradually become part of the mainstream of community development and social policies that focus on local areas. It is standard practice in community development for workers to compile detailed information on local areas and undertaking profiles is a basic ingredient in this process (Henderson and Thomas, 2002). In relation to social policy there has been an increase in the amount of legislation and initiatives (especially since the election of the New Labour government in 1997) that are concerned with tackling social exclusion in disadvantaged areas, building community capacity, devolving decision making in local government and engaging service users and community groups in working in partnership with state and private agencies (Pierson, 2002). Also, the European Union has made community involvement a key focus for its funding of regeneration programmes:

> The focus of urban policy in the UK has widened over the years from a concentration on the physical aspects to a holistic approach which considers the whole range of needs of local communities. Central to this is a 'bottom-up' approach with community development and the use of broadly based partnerships. (Department of Transport, Local Government and the Regions, cited in Smalle and Henderson, 2003, p 124)

Community profiling and appraisals are methods that can be used for identifying the needs of local communities. This applies as much to rural as urban areas and it has been estimated that over 2,000 village appraisals have been carried out in the UK (Allies et al, cited in Francis et al, 2001).

Community profiles

Community profiles can be undertaken by community organisations for a variety of reasons. These include compiling information on the felt or unmet needs of residents, identifying gaps in services and resources, collecting data for funding applications and using the process of collecting information as a means for encouraging citizen participation. Often the exercise is informed by a mixture of these motives. Hawtin and Percy-Smith, the authors of a standard textbook on the subject, define community profiles as:

A comprehensive description of the needs of a population that is defined, or defines itself, as a community, and the resources that exist within that community, carried out with the active involvement of the community itself, for the purpose of developing an action plan or other means of improving the quality of life of the community. (Hawtin and Percy-Smith, 2007, p 10)

They stress that the key elements of a profile should include the comprehensive coverage of needs and issues; identifying resources as well as needs, including skills, networks and informal support; the active involvement of local groups and residents; and the development of an action plan that uses the information collected to improve the quality of life in an area. In practice, the profiles compiled by community organisations may fall short of these aspirations, because of factors such as the lack of technical and human resources and the agendas of local groups being concerned with specific issues. Many local profiles are not comprehensive in their coverage of need and focus on need in relation to specific issues or age groups within an area, such as housing or employment or the needs of young people or senior citizens. Also, it can be challenging for local groups to compile information on the social capital of an area, explained as 'social networks based on shared norms of trust and mutuality' (Gilchrist, 2004, p 4), because of the often opaque and semi-private nature of these relationships.

Community profiles normally combine quantitative and qualitative information from primary and secondary sources. Quantitative information refers to data in a numerical form, such as statistics on the population of an area, whereas qualitative information refers to descriptions of issues, activities and individual or group experiences. Primary sources refer to the collecting of new information from individuals or groups and secondary sources refer to information which already exists. Over recent years there has been a major increase in the volume and range of secondary source information and data on local areas that are electronically published and can be accessed via the internet, including data from the Census, central government departments, local government, health authorities and a host of research bodies. It is now possible to compile a statistical profile of a local area without moving beyond your desk! Of particular relevance to community groups is the data available at the neighbourhood level. This includes the data from IMD and the SOA level data from the Office for National Statistics (ONS), which includes data on population, access to services, community well-being, crime and safety, health and care, income and life styles, work deprivation and the physical environment. A combination of the IMD and ONS data provides a detailed statistical profile of a neighbourhood and some measures of need as defined by normative standards, although care has to be taken in relation to data that have not been revised since the 2001 Census. In addition to this quantitative data there are other secondary sources that can provide information relating to social issues and voluntary activities in an area. These sources can include:

- newspaper reports and articles
- guides to services produced by statutory and voluntary agencies
- annual reports produced by community groups
- minutes of local meetings
- reports produced by local authorities
- local histories
- community studies and fieldwork reports produced by colleges and universities.

Over many years surveys of local communities have provided one of the major means for collecting new information and these can take various forms, including self-completing surveys that are either posted or delivered to households, face-to-face interviewing, telephone and internet surveys. There is a substantial volume of social science literature on how to plan and undertake surveys, including handbooks and guides that are aimed at assisting local community groups, and there are also computer software packages available that assist users in designing a questionnaire and analysing data (Hawtin and Percy-Smith, 2007). Despite the potential access to these resources some community groups, especially those in disadvantaged urban areas, may find undertaking an area-wide survey to be a daunting task, particularly in terms of mobilising the volunteers and technical expertise required to collect data on households and a range of issues relating to the quality of life. These community-wide surveys tend to be carried out more frequently by larger voluntary organisations and local authorities. Community groups are more likely to be reliant on existing sources of data for information on the local population and households, such as data from the IMD and ONS, and to use small-scale or snapshot surveys to collect information on specific issues or the needs of particular groups in an area. Examples are a community centre using a short questionnaire to gather information on the views of the users of its services, or conducting interviews with groups of young people designed to elicit their views on youth provision in an area.

There is a range of other approaches and techniques which can be used in compiling primary source information. These include:

- group discussions
- oral histories
- making short films
- street-based interviews
- the use of photographs, pictures and drawings
- the observation and recording of meetings and community events.

Most of these approaches actively engage with local groups and residents and produce qualitative information and insights into felt need. They are also approaches that have been popularised by what has become known as participatory appraisal.

Participatory appraisal

The term participatory appraisal (PA) covers a range of approaches and techniques that aim to enable local residents and groups to identify their needs, reflect on experiences, make decisions about their priorities and take collective action. PA had its origins in work with rural communities in Latin America and was influenced by the writings and teaching of the Brazilian educator Freire (1972), whose early work on literacy programmes in rural communities was rooted in the radical idea that education had to be related to the daily experiences of poor people and had to be part of a process of critical reflection and 'conscientisation', through which the poor gained an awareness of the exploitative power structures of the wider society and their collective ability to challenge and transform the status quo. PA is extensively used by non-governmental organisations in Latin America, Africa and Asia. Over recent decades, PA approaches and techniques have been adapted and applied to working in North America and Europe. PA is now used by a wide range of voluntary and community organisations in the UK. Some of the communication techniques and exercises derived from PA are used by public bodies, including local authorities, parish councils and health authorities, to inform consultations with service users and local residents. Although PA derives from experiences of southern countries, some of the ideas informing the approach, such as the focus on felt need and resident-led research, have clear connections with a tradition of participatory research in UK adult education and community development (Brookfield, 1983).

There is common ground and some difference in emphasis between community profiles and participatory appraisals. Whereas community profiles normally combine quantitative and qualitative information from primary and secondary sources, PA focuses more exclusively on qualitative information from primary sources and felt definitions of need. Both community profiling and PA share the aim of actively involving residents and groups, but in the PA approach community empowerment, through a process of information gathering, critical reflection and collective action, is placed centre stage:

> The principle behind PA is that the insiders – the people who live on the estate, or the teenagers at the bus shelter for example – are the experts on what is happening in their community. Not only are they the ones with the best information about the problems to be solved. They are also best placed to develop solutions to those problems, and are quite capable of doing so. (Rickford, 2001, p 18)

The PA approach involves supporting and training local residents to do their own information gathering and research. It also places a central emphasis on engaging with those individuals and groups who might be marginalised in local communities, such as young people, members of minority ethnic groups and older people, and who might be hard to reach and reluctant to respond to questionnaires and interviews. The process can involve contacting residents in a variety of public places, such as schools, pubs and bars, community and shopping centres, and using a range of communication techniques and exercises to elicit information about needs and resources, for instance, small group discussions, residents writing their views on flip charts and identifying issues on a local map. It can also involve the use of film and photographs to highlight issues. On the Wood Farm estate in Oxford a local campaign group, which was concerned about the lack of facilities for young people, hired a film maker to work with a group of 20 young people to make a 50-minute film about their experiences of living in the area and their views on provision for young people. A number of the young people had been excluded from school and had experience of the youth justice system and were considered to be 'trouble makers' by many adults in the local community. The young people defined the agenda for the film, assisted with the filming, were involved in the editing and helped to front the public launch of the film. The project attracted considerable attention from the media and contributed to the local authority eventually agreeing to fund a new youth centre for the estate (Beebee, 2005).

The PA approach has a number of potential strengths in relation to identifying need. These include the focus on felt need, the 'know how' and informal contacts of local researchers and the use of a range of written and non-verbal techniques to capture the experiences of marginalised groups in the local area. The potential limitations include the demands made on local volunteers and the challenging and time-consuming task of collating views and experiences from a variety of different sources. Community profiles, particularly those which cover the whole of an area, are likely to produce a broader and more substantial range of quantitative data, whereas appraisals help to get 'under the skin' of a community and produce insights into informal networks and the quality of interpersonal relationships. In an ideal world both approaches should be used to build up a well-rounded picture of local areas.

Finally it should be noted that needs are often identified without the use of profiles and appraisals. The history of community action in the UK is full of examples, particularly in relation to housing and planning issues, of felt need being expressed through petitions, complaints to local councils and protest action (for example Henderson et al, 1982). In these situations information gathering in local areas tends to become an exercise in documenting the impact of issues and providing data to back up collective action. The rational model of collecting information, reflecting on the results and devising action plans does not always fit with the realities of everyday life.

Skills for identifying need

The knowledge and skills that inform the work of paid staff and volunteers in identifying need, can be broadly divided into the specialist knowledge and skills relating to the approaches and methods being used to compile information, and knowledge and skills that can be considered to be generic to undertaking community development in local areas. Good practice indicates that training is vital before community profiles or appraisals are undertaken. Hawtin and Percy-Smith (2007) recommend that staff and volunteers need to attend courses that will cover such issues as the organisation of surveys, interviewing techniques, recording responses, confidentiality and personal safety. In a similar vein staff and volunteers involved in PA will need to receive training that addresses the philosophy underpinning the approach and the various methods, communication techniques and exercises that can be used to elicit information and engage with local groups and residents.

Profiles and appraisals should be part of a wider developmental process that involves increasing the levels of citizen participation, engaging with marginalised groups, informal learning and collective action. Facilitating and enabling this process has traditionally been a key role for paid community workers and requires a complex set of skills and a detailed knowledge of both local issues and social policy at the UK level. As community development has moved towards acquiring a more distinct occupational status, the generic skills required to undertake this work have been defined in more detail. The National Occupational Standards for Community Development Work (Paulo, 2002) identify 21 core skills for staff employed in neighbourhoods and relate these skills to six key roles:

- developing working relationships with communities and organisations;
- encouraging people to work with and learn from each other;
- work with people in communities to plan for change and take collective action;
- work with people in communities to develop and use frameworks for evaluation;
- develop community organisations;
- reflect and develop their own practice and roles.

The skills required to perform these roles underpin the development work involved in preparing profiles and appraisals. For instance, 'developing working relationships with communities and organisations' involves applying skills in communication, relationship building and networking with a range of local residents, community groups and statutory bodies.

Are skills and technical knowledge enough to make a good community development worker? There is some evidence, from small-scale studies, which suggests that the personality traits and qualities of the worker or volunteer can be as important as skills. In her study of networking Gilchrist reports on the reflections of a panel of 11 community development workers and concludes that: 'Personality traits seem to have a significant impact on networking ability. These include a commitment to perceive and value the whole person, showing interest, empathy and attention' (Gilchrist, 2004, p 5).

Gilchrist identifies the qualities which make for a good networker – affability, integrity, audacity, adaptability and tenacity. These qualities echo the findings from an earlier study, which reported on how 16 community leaders in Glasgow evaluated community workers:

> Almost without exception, the local activists stressed personal qualities as being the foundation for good community work and the qualities which were emphasised were those which could help local people overcome their inhibitions about becoming involved in collective action. These inhibitions – low expectations, fear of authority, apathy, a personal view of the world – could be counteracted by workers who displayed the opposite characteristic: optimism, high expectations, a collectivist view of the world, a lack of deference to authority, coupled with the virtues of hard work, reliability and determination. (Bryant and Bryant, 1982, p 7)

Community workers who are resident in the local areas where they work are normally better placed to pick up on felt needs and emerging issues than are staff members who live elsewhere. Although there can be considerable tensions over maintaining professional and personal boundaries (Henderson and Thomas, 2002), becoming part of the everyday life of an area can enable a worker to gain a more detailed and sharper insight into informal networks and the interactions between groups. This local knowledge can include first-hand experiences of behaviour that has a negative and destructive impact on community life, such as crime, racism and drug abuse, as well as providing social links that can positively assist with development work.

Conclusion

Identifying need in local areas is now part of the mainstream of UK social policy. Sophisticated normative measures are being used by central and local government and many other agencies to target extra resources to localities. For community organisations and enterprises these policies have been a mixed blessing. Those groups located in areas that score high in the league tables of the IMD have normally benefited from access to new funding and infrastructure support, while groups located outside or on the fringe of priority areas tend to struggle for extra resources. An inherent limitation of area-based anti-poverty strategies is that the majority of disadvantaged households are not always concentrated in a handful of localities but are scattered, with varying degrees of concentration, over a wider area in many towns and cities.

Community organisations are now much better placed to undertake their own assessments of local needs. Compared with 10 years ago, more statistical data is available at the neighbourhood level, information from local government is more readily available, the internet has opened up access to a mass of research material on local communities, there is more advice available on how to compile community profiles and PA has generated new ideas and experiences in relation to identifying felt needs. Despite these developments many community groups may still find it a major challenge to map the needs of their local areas, because of such factors as a lack of volunteers, the demands on time and resources and the absence of advice and support from community workers and other professionals. Also, community leaders in some areas may be cynical about the credibility of profiles and PA programmes, based on previous experiences of the evidence from surveys not being used and acted on by the relevant authorities.

Identifying felt need is only the first stage in what can be a long and tortuous process of improving social conditions and the quality of life in local areas. To be effective in translating felt need into expressed need and achieving results requires community groups and social entrepreneurs to have the organisational capacity to link and integrate information gathering, informal learning and the ability to take collective action. All four case studies in this volume show the importance of identifying need, and both the Indian and US studies clearly show that need is not something that remains static and that interventions and the focus of projects and organisations need to change in response to developing perceived need.

References

Active Community Unit (1999) *Report of the policy action team on community self help*, London: Home Office.

Association of Public Health Observatories (2008) *A profile of the nation's health*, London: Department of Health.

Beebee, S. (2005) 'The Wood Farm audit', *The Edge*, issue 10, The National Youth Agency, p 7.

Bradshaw, J. (1972) ' The concept of social need', in M. Fitzgerald, P. Halmos, J. Muncie, D. Zeldin (eds) *Welfare in action*, London: Routledge and Kegan Paul, pp 33-36.

Brookfield, S. (1983) *Adult learners, adult education and the community*, Milton Keynes: Open University Press.

Bryant, B. (1989) 'Pinehurst People's Centre', in *Community*, vol 10, no 4, National Federation of Community Organisations, p 4.

Bryant, B. and Bryant, R. (1982) 'What makes a good community worker?', *Community Work*, Association of Community Workers, p 7.

Chanan, G. (2004) *Measures of community*, London: Community Development Foundation.

Community Development Foundation (2006) *The community development challenge*, London: CDF Publications.

Dench, G., Gavron, K. and Young, M. (2006) *The New East End; kinship, race and conflict*, London: Profile Books Ltd.

Dorling, D., Rigby, J., Wheeler, B., Ballos, D., Thomas, B., Fahmy, E., Gordon, D. and Lupton, R. (2007) *Poverty, wealth and place in Britain, 1968 to 2005*, Bristol: The Policy Press.

Doyal, L. and Gough, I. (1991) *A theory of human needs*, Basingstoke: MacMillan.

Flaherty, J., Veit-Wilson, J. and Dornan, P. (2004) *Poverty: The fact*, London: Child Poverty Action Group.

Francis, D., Henderson, P. and Derounian, J. (2001) *Community development and rural issues*, London: Community Development Foundation.

Freire, P. (1972) *Pedagogy of the oppressed*, Harmondsworth: Penguin Books.

Fried, A. and Elman, R. (eds) (1971) *Charles Booth's London*, Harmondsworth: Pelican Books.

Gilchrist, A. (2004) *The well-connected community*, Bristol: The Policy Press.

Hawtin, M. and Percy-Smith, J. (2007) *Community profiling: A practical guide*, Maidenhead: Open University Press.

Henderson, P. and Thomas, D. (2002) *Skills in neighbourhood work*, Abingdon: Routledge.

Henderson, P., Wright, A. and Wyncoll, K. (eds) (1982) *Success and struggles on council estates*, London: Association of Community Workers.

HM Treasury and Cabinet Office (2007) *The future role of the third sector in social and economic regeneration: Final report*, Norwich: The Stationery Office.

Leat, D. (1975) 'Social theory and the historical construction of social work activity: the role of Samuel Barnett,' in P. Leonard (ed) *The sociology of community action*, Stoke-on-Trent: University of Staffordshire, pp 24-37.

Mayo, M. and Robertson, J. (2003) 'The historical and policy context; setting the scene for current debates', in S. Banks, H. Butcher, P. Henderson and J. Robertson (eds) *Managing community practice*, Bristol: The Policy Press, pp 23-34.

Milligan, F. (1961) 'Community associations and centres', in P. Kuenstler (ed) *Community organization in Britain*, London: Faber, pp 97-116.

NCSS (National Council of Social Service) (1950) *Our neighbourhood*, London: NCSS.

Neighbourhood Renewal Unit (2001) *A new commitment to neighbourhood renewal: A national strategy action plan*, London: Office of the Deputy Prime Minister.

Office of the Deputy Prime Minister (2004) *The English indices of social deprivation*, London: ODPM.

O'Malley, J. (1977) *The politics of community action*, Nottingham: Spokesman Books.

Paulo (2002) *The national occupational standards for community development work*, Grantham; Paulo.

Pierson, J. (2002) *Tackling social exclusion*, Abingdon: Routledge.

Popple, K. (1995) *Analysing community work*, Buckingham: Open University Press.

Rickford, F. (2001) 'Right up your street', *Community Care*, 18-24 January, pp 18-19.

Smalle, Y. and Henderson, P. (2003) 'The manager's role in community auditing', in S. Banks, H. Butcher, P. Henderson and J. Robertson (eds) *Managing community practice*, Bristol: The Policy Press, pp 123-36.

FIVE

Stakeholder participation and involvement in social enterprises

Chris Durkin and Robert Gunn

Introduction

> Go to the people. Live with them. Learn from them. Start with what they know. Build with what they have. But with the best leaders, when the work is done, the task accomplished, the people will say 'we have done this ourselves'. Lao Tzu (c 600 BC to 531 BC)

The above observation can also be true of the very people who become representatives of the community or a service user group, because by being involved in the design and potential running of a service an individual may become separated from their constituency. In other words there is a need to look at the issue of legitimacy. Despite these limitations, involving stakeholders in the development and running of an organisation can have considerable benefits, it can:

- help in the identification of need and targeting of services;
- help in the design and structuring of services;
- ensure the organisation remains focused on the needs of the service user group, preventing the organisation from 'drifting';
- ensure the organisation is accountable;
- ensure the organisation's management structure is representative of the beneficiaries;
- provide feedback as to the quality of services (Improvement and Development Agency for local government, 2009).

The involvement of stakeholders can help in the drawing up of the organisation's vision, mission and goals at the start of an evaluation process. In turn the stakeholders can provide invaluable information about how a service is working. For instance, how a user experiences a service may reduce organisational drift and ensure managers remain focused on the organisational values and aims.

This chapter addresses the centrality of stakeholder involvement in third sector organisations and the need for management to take account of a number of different 'audiences'. Service user and stakeholder participation in the design, delivery and management of third sector organisations is seen as of crucial importance. The chapter is divided into four sections. First we look at the social policy context of stakeholder participation, looking at its developing position and current emphasis on consultation. The second section locates social enterprises within this policy context, focusing in particular on the links between social enterprises and communities. The third section looks at the issue of power and how this underpins many of the issues facing organisations, and the final section develops the concept of stakeholder participation in an organisational and managerial context.

Social policy context

Before looking at why the organisational imperatives of stakeholder involvement are so important we need to put it into context. In previous chapters the authors have looked at the development of social enterprises in the 19th century at a time when the economy could be seen as liberal, with the UK government's role 'to provide a firmly established and clearly understood framework within which society could very largely run itself' (Thane, 1990, p 1, cited in Stewart, 2007, p 26).

We can also see that in the period 1948 to 1979 the government's role became significant both in terms of the setting up of a 'welfare state' but also in its control of certain economic sectors like steel, telecommunications and coal. Although there was, during this period, a broad belief in Keynesian economics and an agreement that the state had a significant role to play (Page, 2007), the ideological differences revolved around the extent of private provision. The situation changed in the 1980s following the election of Margaret Thatcher as Prime Minister in 1979. She and a number of her colleagues had been heavily influenced by the Chicago economist Milton Friedman and the writings of Hayek. The newly elected Conservative administration had a belief that the country's economic problems were down to the state sector playing too significant a role and, in their view, would benefit from an injection of private sector management culture.

The Thatcher government presented a critique of inefficient public sector organisations that would benefit from the rigours of the private sector; in particular, a stress on markets, private sector management and a much greater voice for the consumer. The emphasis was on the '3 Es' of economy, efficiency and effectiveness, with economic value being seen as of central importance and organisations being exhorted to be customer focused, a prelude to the current emphasis on stakeholder involvement.

Although the election of Tony Blair and New Labour in 1997 did not lead to a change in the neo-liberal ideology, it was 'tempered', however, by the influence of Communitarian thinking – a counter to the individualised emphasis of the Conservatives. Calder (2004) argues that there are two basic features of this: first the importance of community and second the importance of civil society, with the emphasis on association and the voluntary and community sector. Within this context the importance of rights, responsibilities to others and the need for active citizens were highlighted. Rights and responsibilities were in large part about the rights of people to participate and for governments and organisations to consult. Developing civil society and particularly the third sector within this context was seen as very important.

In social policy terms there was no real major ideological change between the Conservative and Labour governments; the significant difference was not in terms of who provided services but in terms of focus, in particular the importance of targeting welfare provision to those most in need. Some have gone so far as to describe the moves that have taken place as the development of a 'Hollow State', reflecting the decline of the state as a provider and deliverer of services and the rise of the private sector, voluntary organisations and social enterprises (Fredericksen and London, 2000). The emphasis on who provides the services is now seen as less important; what is seen as crucial is finding the most appropriate provider. In this context the procurement and commissioning policies of local government become the pivot on which welfare service delivery hangs together; they provide the structure and an environment for the development of services. In terms of actual delivery, the government's role has changed, remaining as a provider in areas such as education and health, as well as the provider of statutory services in child protection and mental health, while being a commissioner and purchaser of other services. It is within this changing landscape that UK social enterprises have developed.

Alongside the more structural changes taking place there has been a change in emphasis in areas such as health and social care, with greater importance being given to a more 'preventative' agenda. In part this has been a response to rising societal issues like obesity and drug abuse, but also because along with a more community focused agenda and the view that communities need to be 'empowered' goes an implicit recognition that people need to have more 'control' over the development of services. The expansion of the third sector in recent years has been driven by demand in areas such as adult social care, which in part has been 'engineered' by government policy in order to reduce the role of the state and develop a culture in which organisations compete to provide services. Within this context the government's role is to commission and procure services from whichever organisation is deemed to offer best value, a term that suggests the criteria for commissioning is not based purely on the economic cost.

Stakeholder and service user involvement is now a key component of much of the UK government's thinking on welfare provision, grounded on the reshaping of welfare services and the building up of social capital. These policy developments have also been supported by a developing legislative framework in areas of welfare provision such as mental health, community care and children and families, as well as in a broader human rights framework that came into place when the 1998 Human Rights Act was introduced. The involvement of service users is now a feature of both policy and practice (Beresford et al, 2005).

The UK government has also supported the development of social enterprises, for instance by developing regulations governing the setting up of community interest companies, which include a 'community interest test' and 'asset lock', to ensure the companies are '… established for community purposes and the assets and profits are dedicated to these purposes' (www.cicregulator.gov.uk/index. shtml). Effectively stakeholder involvement is now enshrined in legislation, with community interest companies being required '… to formally report directly to an independent body on the extent to which they [are] involving stakeholders in their activities and therefore account for any lack of activity in this area of their operations' (Low and Cowton, 2004, p 47).

Although the language of autonomy, empowerment, participation and partnership may all be suggestive of inclusion the reality may well be tokenistic, lacking any real involvement in decision making, limited to 'consultation exercises' and service evaluations that merely evaluate the quality of service provision. In addition, although the Labour government places a great deal of emphasis on 'empowering' communities to identify problems and needs, the government is often seen as prescriptive. In the UK, for instance, Charles Leadbeater argues that the 'Government has to become molecular: it has to get into the bloodstream of society, not impose change or deliver solutions from without. Government is exercised in a myriad of micro settings, and often not just by state employees but by teachers, experts, advisers, parents, volunteers and peers' (Leadbeater, 2004, p 89). He goes even further and argues for the need for 'personalisation', which he describes as an idea that puts '… users at the heart of services, enabling them to become participants in the design and delivery'. In this way, '… services will be more effective by mobilising millions of people as co-producers of the public goods they value' (Leadbeater, 2004, p 19).

The government is increasingly emphasising the personalised agenda in areas such as adult social care by introducing individualised care budgets. The aims of the personalisation agenda are very much about providing choice for users and allowing them to be involved in the decision-making process. Ultimately users are seen as playing a crucial role in developing services, emphasising a 'bottom-up' approach in contrast to the top-down hierarchical approach of a state system.

The personalisation agenda is a participatory approach, which contrasts with much of welfare provision in the 20th century, when the professionally qualified practitioner was central to delivery of services. In the personalised approach the user is at the centre, ultimately being in charge of their individualised care. It is seen as an approach that connects the individual with the collective and in so doing allows the political right to argue that it is a 'consumerist approach' and for the left to see it as providing citizens with greater control and a louder voice (Leadbeater et al, 2008, pp 80-1). Leadbeater argues that the personalisation approach leads to service users becoming 'co-producers', by which he means they are actively involved in care, rather than 'passive' recipients. Personalisation, Leadbeater believes, can operate on five different levels:

1. providing users with more customer focused services;
2. providing users with more say in 'navigating' through services;

3. giving users more control over how resources are allocated;
4. users are actively involved in the design and provision of services;
5. 'self-organisation' of services (Leadbetter 2004, pp 21-24).

At the fifth level the author feels 'Public service professionals would help to create platforms and environments, peer-to-peer support networks, which allow people to devise these solutions collaboratively' (Leadbetter, 2004, p 24). This latter approach is focused largely on the community being 'empowered' to find solutions for societal problems.

The emphasis on community empowerment and involvement assumes that communities are homogenous places, whereas in reality they are made up of diverse groups of residents with multiple identities. People are not involved with merely one community but a number of different communities reflecting the complexity of their lives and interests. What is important is the development of social capital (the development of supportive community networks). There is a recognition that in areas where social exclusion is seen to be an issue, social networks are weak, which in policy terms is part of the reason why the government has placed so much emphasis on people becoming 'active citizens'.

Where do social enterprises fit within this changing landscape?

In earlier chapters we have seen that the vision of the social entrepreneur is crucial to the success of the organisation. In setting up an organisation the founder needs to have a clear view of their aims. Understanding the social and organisational vision of the social entrepreneur is, however, only one aspect of analysis. The vision needs to be grounded in reality, that is, the vision must be based on a recognised need that in turn is located in a specific community. To understand needs a social entrepreneur has to understand the micro position but also have a view of the wider macro context. However, from a third sector perspective, as Eikenberry and Klover, (2004, p 33) argue, '... to understand the internal attitudes and behaviors of nonprofit organizations, one must understand the external environment and its pressures on an organization'. Bloom and Dees (2008) take this further by adopting an 'ecosytems framework', arguing that if social entrepreneurs are:

> [t]o create significant and long-lasting changes, social entrepreneurs must understand and often alter the social system that creates and sustains the problems in the first place. This social system includes all of the actors – the friends, foes, competitors, and even the innocent bystanders – party to the problem, as well as the larger environment – the laws, policies, social norms, demographic trends, and cultural institutions – within which the actors play. (Bloom and Dees, 2008, p 47)

Social enterprises, therefore, are more than enterprises with social aims. Pearce, for example, defined six characteristics fundamental to social enterprise:

1. having a social purpose or purposes;
2. achieving the social purposes by, at least in part, engaging in trade in the marketplace; such as job creation, training or provision of local services, to be directly involved in producing goods or providing services to a market;
3. not distributing profits to individuals;
4. holding assets and wealth in trust for community benefit;
5. democratically involving members of its constituency in the governance of the organisation; and governance and ownership structures, based on participation by clients, users, local community groups or trustees. Profits are distributed to stakeholders or for the benefit of the community;
6. being independent organisations accountable to a defined constituency and to the wider community (Pearce, 2003, p 4).

Defourny and Nyssens, in turn, summarise social enterprises as follows:

> Social enterprises are not-for-profit private organizations providing goods or services directly related to their explicit aim to benefit the community. They rely on a collective dynamics involving various types of stakeholders in their governing bodies, they place a high value on their autonomy and they bear economic risks linked to their activity. (Defourny and Nyssens, 2008, p 5)

These definitions are important because they stress the role of social enterprises as being part of the development of civil society and communities. In the four case studies in this volume we can see the fact that social entrepreneurs cannot work in isolation but are part of significant networks, and account must always be taken of the views of stakeholders.

The state's role has now shifted significantly in many countries, such that Alcock (2008), focusing on the UK, talks about the governance of social policy. This has been particularly apparent in the UK in terms of the delivery of services, where there has been a move away from central control to services that are more responsive to needs of consumers or service users and that involve local communities. In terms of actual delivery there is an emphasis on partnership. In April 2009 a legal duty was placed on councils in England to 'inform, consult and involve' local people. But how do you ensure that the 'voice' of the majority is 'heard' and not the usual well-connected individuals (Pitchford et al, 2009)? We have seen in Richard Bryant's chapter how using a community development approach can help identify need. Such an approach from an organisational perspective has considerable merit. Compiling a community profile (sometimes referred to as 'community auditing' and community planning) can provide a picture of the nature, needs and resources of a community ideally drawn up with the active participation of that community. We can also see it is a useful first stage in any community planning process, establishing a framework that is widely agreed. Within this context disciplines like marketing have become very significant, marketing being '… understood as both a search for what consumers value and a device for building ongoing relationships with customers' (Moore, 1995, p 66).

The notion of governance has in all sectors, to varying degrees, led to the managerial role becoming wider, and the need for account to be taken of stakeholders' perspective has grown. Spear et al use the definition of governance to mean '… the systems and processes concerned with ensuring the overall direction, supervision and accountability of an organisation' (Spear et al, 2007, p 6).

Stakeholder participation and involvement

Stakeholders are talked about throughout this chapter. So far, we have seen both the importance given to stakeholder engagement by both government and organisations, and we have also seen that service users are significant stakeholders. In a business model service users are the 'main' customers and for any organisation that is customer focused, involving service users in the design, delivery and management of services is very important. However, seeing service users as synonymous with stakeholders is to ignore the fact that 'Stakeholders are those groups who have a stake in or claim on the [organisation]' (Freeman, 2001, p 102).

Helmut K. Anheier (2000, p 6) argues that private sector companies have only one 'bottom line' of profit maximisation whereas the management challenge for third sector organisations '… is that they have several, and some would say "sometimes too many"'. A third sector organisation has multiple bottom lines, requiring managers to take account not only of service users but other stakeholder interest, which may include staff, volunteers, referring agencies (for example, health and social care organisations), local politicians, the police or funders. Spear et al point out that there are sometimes difficulties managing the competing demands of different stakeholders (Spear et al 2007, p 9). Low and Cowton (2004), argue that even in the private sector there has been a significant shift in emphasis away from a purely profit-oriented approach, with many companies adopting a stakeholder management strategy, which the authors divide into two forms: engagement and participation, with the latter requiring active stakeholder involvement by, for instance, membership of a company board of directors.

As is shown in Chapter Nine, there has been increasing recognition of the need for leaders and managers to adopt a more inclusive outward facing mode of management, in which there is awareness of the needs of the market. Moullin (2002, pp 99-100) identifies some 'fundamental concepts' for managing organisations that are relevant to the present discussion and are as follows:

- customer focus – service user focus;
- leadership and constancy of purpose – vision and mission – are defined: refers to long-term commitment by the senior management;

- people development and involvement – training and developing staff as well as involving staff in the decision-making processes;
- partnership development – partnership working with both service users, stakeholders and other agencies;
- management by fact – decisions are based on facts, not just staff opinion;
- continuous learning – analyse results and performance and use this information to improve processes;
- innovation and improvement – when evaluating a service;
- public responsibility – need not only to satisfy service users but also be a responsible employer;
- results orientation – satisfying the needs of all relevant stakeholders, for example staff, service users, partners etc.

Identifying who the key stakeholders are is a major part of both a general planning process and the development of a marketing strategy. As a result a number of 'stakeholder analysis models' have identified tools to help focus on the stakeholders to which we need to give particular attention (see for example, Copeman, 2009 and www.mindtools.com/pages/article/newPPM_07.htm).

Organisations do not work in isolation; they are interdependent and have to work in 'partnership' with each other. This is particularly relevant for social enterprises that work in health and social care, where there is increasing emphasis on multidisciplinary working. It is important to identify other interested groups; locating those stakeholders who are the most significant, as well as illustrating the fact that any organisation needs to take account of other wider interest groups. Service users may be seen to be key stakeholders who need to participate in decision making, but so may be the local authority because they are providing a grant. In this process service users' power may be seen to be less than that of a funding local authority. Decisions may need to be made to invest resources in 'empowering' users. For instance, in a disability project, users may find it difficult to 'articulate' their views and may therefore need help although the provision of advocates to ensure their 'voice' is heard. Each stakeholder has specific needs; a factor which will influence how an organisation 'targets' its constituencies.

What a stakeholder analysis shows is the power of interests groups. This is also apparent in a wider context, when a social enterprise 'forms' a partnership with others to deliver a service. Partners could be from the third sector, the public sector or the private sector. Each partner will have their own agenda and reasons for becoming involved, a private company may become involved because the partnership provides it with a link to a customer base, a third sector organisation may get involved because it is the only way that they could obtain a grant or because they are too small to deliver a particular service, whereas the public sector may become involved as part of a wider governmental strategy. Eikenberry and Kluver suggest that the increasing 'marketisation' of social enterprises and increasing emphasis on raising revenue may reduce the need to build up traditional networks with their stakeholders. As the authors state, '... stakeholders who were once donors or members become consumers or clients, and the focus of the organization shifts from creating networks of trust to creating opportunities for selling more products or services to individuals' (Eikenberry and Kluver, 2004, p 137). Analysing the organisational environment and identifying stakeholders is a key aspect of planning, management and leadership. We would also argue that being 'in touch' with your constituency prevents organisational drift and ensures the organisation remains focused on their mission. This could be an issue for social enterprises, where an emphasis on profit could undermine social aims.

Power

Partnerships, participation and service user involvement are not static concepts but active processes, which involve negotiation and the operation of power. To understand how stakeholders can shape the way a social enterprise operates we need to understand what power is and the basis for each stakeholder group's influence in the relationships they have with each other.

Although a contested concept, power has been generally defined by Weber (1972) as the probability of persons or groups carrying out their will even when opposed by others. The conventional view has the state and its operation of power at the centre and Weber was particularly concerned with 'the independent powers of bureaucratic forms of organisation' (Pinch, 1985, p 36). His perspective suggests that decisions taken by officials in bureaucracies tend to support the survival of the organisation rather than respond to the desires of other stakeholders. Weber was concerned that bureaucracies were becoming more powerful than the governments or institutions they were designed to serve. He felt that managers given legitimate power by their place in the bureaucracy would always support the existence and influence of the bureaucratic structure, rather than respond to the desires of policy makers who set out what organisations are for, and users or 'customers' of the organisation. Weber describes a hierarchy of offices, with communication channelled through them, spheres of authority determined by general rules and governed by regulations that resemble traditional government welfare departments. The concentration of power that this implies restricts influence on policy (Weber, 1972; Collins, 1987; Holton and Turner, 1989; Parkin, 1991; Lassman and Speirs, 1994). The structure of a social enterprise may be a significant factor, with power concentrated in the hands of a 'founder' who may find it difficult to involve others in the management of an organisation; a problem that becomes particularly acute when the founder wishes to 'stand down' – the so-called 'Founder Syndrome' (Spear et al, 2007).

Classical thinkers like Taylor and Weber saw organisations in a rational sense and bureaucracies as the most rational and efficient organisational form, in which everything could be broken down into its constituent parts. There may be some merit in this approach in that organisations need specialists and in certain cases need hierarchically organised structures, particularly when organisations become large and complex. This apparent logical analysis of organisational structure, however, fails to take account of people's motivations.

Weber's theories do not help us much in this regard, but Lukes (1976) develops a 'three-dimensional view of power', an account of the exercise of power in organisations.

The **one-dimensional view of power** is a focus on behaviour, decision making, key issues, observable (overt) conflict and subjective interests, seen as preferences revealed by participation. One group has the power to threaten sanctions or invoke an implicit threat to maintain power. It can be seen when group A can succeed in affecting what group B does.

The **two-dimensional view of power** is a qualified critique of the behavioural focus, which examines decision making and non-decision making, issues and potential issues, observable (overt or covert) conflict and subjective interests seen as preferences or grievances. It shows that the way that debates are shaped by what is seen as reasonable and realistic are important factors in maintaining authority.

The **three-dimensional view of power** is a fundamental critique of the behavioural focus, which is concerned with decision making and control over the organisational agenda, issues and potential issues, observable (overt or covert) and latent conflict and subjective and real issues. The shape of the organisation is an important factor in the decision-making process, where the socially constructed and culturally patterned behaviour of groups and the practices of institutions are implicitly connected to the exercise of power. Power is seen as a function of collective forces and social arrangements where bias results from the form of the organisation.

By incorporating the work of Dahl, who examined decision making in pluralist settings where members of minority groups maintain their independent cultural traditions, Lukes provides a more sophisticated analysis. It includes the ability of the powerful to define the agenda and shape preferences and is relevant within this context for third sector organisations working in 'partnership' with more powerful public and private sector organisations. Lukes develops an analysis of the complexities of power relationships between stakeholder groups. He shows that their relationships operate at more than one level and that power cannot be viewed as the simple exercise of force to pursue goals but the ability of the powerful to control the agenda. In this way, the status quo is maintained without any overt threat or even questions being raised about the way that the debate has been framed. Stakeholders may not be aware that their behaviour has been influenced and will not have experienced conflict. This view is pertinent because it highlights the limited power that some people may have and also recognises the difficulties that may accrue in partnership working with different qualities of relationship existing between strategic levels and operational levels.

Levin (1997) advocates a concentration on intent and appraisal using three manifestations of power that are derived from Lukes. He has identified the three types of power that are used in the policy-making process: power to do, power over and power to achieve:

- **power to do** – literally what an individual is actually able to do, to make a decision alone;
- **power over** – the power of an individual or group over another individual or group to direct their actions or behaviour;
- **power to achieve** – the power to realise one's will and determine that a policy will incorporate at least some of the characteristics desired by the power holder.

Foucault (1980, 1991) contends that at the macro level the conventional state and pressure group configuration is no longer able to provide sufficient explanations of the operation of power. He breaks through the notion of monopoly powers by the state to real problems of governance. Foucault's ideas contribute to the interpretation of the nuances of stakeholder relationships: how people's contact with other stakeholders (users, managers, politicians, funders, workers and volunteers) may influence them, or how people are influenced and how this shapes their perceptions of the social enterprise (Rainbow, 1984; Merquior, 1991).

Understanding power enables us to analyse and think about relationships between people and organisations. Within this context the notion of participation and partnership is important. However, it must be acknowledged that so often consultation processes are 'tokenistic' in that the participants are merely going through the motions rather than being involved in a process in which they feel empowered. Because the essence of partnership working involves the exchange of power, it is important to get a sense of what participation means. Sherry Arnstein's 'ladder of citizen participation' (Arnstein 1969), gives an idea of how 'participation' can occur in practice and shows that some stakeholders can be more involved in the exercise of power than others. What we can see in ChapterThirteen (India case study) is that there is sometimes a complex interplay between the micro and macro environments with, for instance, the wider market conditions affecting organisational development and the users.

If 'participation' or 'empowerment' are about the transfer of power as Cowden and Singh (2007) point out, we need to consider how realistic it is to expect people who are oppressed and marginalised to challenge '… the circumstances in which they exist' (Cowden and Singh, 2007,p 17).This may also lead to false expectations on behalf of policy makers whose idea of 'partnership working' is effectively empowering '… those who expect to get the most in the first place, at the same time as it disempowers those with the lowest expectations' (Cowden and Singh, 2007,p 7). The danger is that with this view users become merely 'consultants rather than activists' and '… simply incorporated into an agenda dominated by performance management, audit and evaluation' (Cowden and Singh, 2007, p 20).

Conclusion

In looking at how an organisation is managed we can see the potential complexity of involving stakeholders in the running of an organisation, particularly as an organisation grows in size. The question that remains, however, is how do you ensure that an organisation does not 'disconnect' from its roots and from its constituency? Although Anheir (2000) argues that third sector organisations are the most complex to manage because of their multiple stakeholders, the fundamental principles of good management and leadership remain. In all successful organisations managers need to understand their markets, whether that be for sport, bread or cars. Losing sight of the needs of your constituency will guarantee failure.

References

Alcock, P. (2008) *Social Policy in Britain* (3rd edn), Basingstoke: Palgrave Macmillan.

Anheier, H. K. (2000) 'Managing non-profit organisations: towards a new approach', *Civil Society Working Paper 1* (www.lse.ac.uk/collections/CCS/publications/cswp/civil_society_wp.htm).

Arnstein, S. (1969) 'A ladder of citizen participation', *Journal of the American Institute of Planners*, vol 35, no 4, pp 216-24.

Beresford, P., Shamash. M., Forrest, V., Turner, M. and Branfield, F. (2005) *Developing social care: Service users' vision for adult support*, SCIE Report 7, London: Social Care Institute for Excellence (www.scie.org.uk/publications/reports/report07.asp).

Bloom, P. N. and Dees, J. G. (2008) 'Cultivate your ecosystem', article originally published in *Stanford Social Innovation Review*, Winter, pp 47-53 (www.caseatduke.org/news/1207/Dees_Bloom_Ecosystem.html#cultivateecosystem).

Calder, G. (2004) 'Communitarianism and New Labour', Electronic Journal: *Social Issues* , vol 2, no 1 (www.whb.co.uk/socialissues/indexvol2.htm).

Collins, R. (1987) *Webarian sociological theory*, Cambridge: Cambridge University Press.

Copeman, C. (2009) *Stakeholder matrix* (PowerPoint), KnowHow NonProfit (www.knowhownonprofit.org/organisation/strategy/directionsetting/stakeholdermatrix.ppt/view).

Cowden, S. and Singh, G. (2007) 'The "user": friend, foe or fetish?: a critical exploration of user involvement in health and social care', *Critical Social Policy*, vol 27, no 1, pp 5-23.

Defourny, J. and Nyssens, M. (eds.) (2008) 'Social enterprise in Europe: recent trends and developments', *EMES Working Papers no. 08/01* (www.emes.net/fileadmin/emes/PDF_files/News/2008/WP_08_01_SE_WEB.pdf).

Eikenberry, A. and Kluver, J. (2004) 'The marketization of the nonprofit sector: civil society at risk?', *Public Administration Review*, March/April, vol 64, no 2, pp 132-40.

Foucault, M. (1980) *Power/knowledge*, London: Harvester Wheatsheaf.

Foucault, M. (1991) *Discipline and punish*, London: Penguin.

Fredericksen, P. and London, R. (2000) 'Disconnect in the Hollow State: the pivotal role of organizational capacity in community-based development organizations', *Public Administration Review*, vol 60, pp 230–39 (www.accessmylibrary.com/coms2/summary_0286-623200_ITM).

Freeman, R. (2001). 'A stakeholder theory of the modern corporation,' in M. Snoeyenbos, R. Almeder and J. Humber (eds) *Business ethics* (3rd edn), New York: Prometheus Books, pp 101-14.

Holton, R. and Turner, B. (1989) *Max Weber on economy and society*, London: Routledge.

Improvement and Development Agency for local government (2009) *Identifying and involving stakeholders* (http://makingendsmeet.idea.gov.uk/idk/core/page.do?pageId=5149018).

Lassman, P. and Speirs, R. (eds) (1994) *Weber: Political writings*, Cambridge: Cambridge University Press.

Leadbeater, C. (2004) *Personalisation through participation: A new script for public services*, London: Demos.

Leadbeater, C., Bartlett, J. and Gallagher, N. (2008) *Making it personal*, London: Demos.

Levin, P. (1997) *Making social policy*, Buckingham: Open University Press.

Low, C. and Cowton, C. (2004) 'Beyond stakeholder engagement: the challenges of stakeholder participation in corporate governance', *International Journal of Business Governance and Ethics*, vol 1, no 1, pp 45-55.

Lukes, S. (1976) *Power: A radical view*, London: Macmillan Press.

Merquior, J. (1991) *Foucault*, Hammersmith: Fontana.

Moore, M. (1995) *Creating public value*, Cambridge: Harvard University Press.

Moullin, M. (2002) *Delivering excellence in health and social care*, Maidenhead: Open University Press.

Page, R. (2007) *Revisiting the welfare state*, Maidenhead: Open University Press.

Parkin, F. (1991) *Max Weber*, London: Routledge.

Pearce, J. (2003) *Social enterprise in anytown*, London: Calouste Gulbenkian Foundation.

Pinch, S. (1985) *Cities and services*, London: Routledge and Keegan Paul.

Pitchford, M., Archer, T. with Ramsden, S. (2009) *The duty to involve: Making it work*, London: Community Development Foundation.

Rainbow, P. (ed) (1984) *The Foulcault reader*, London: Peregrine.

Spear, R., Cornforth, C. and Aitken, M. (2007) *For love and money: Governance and social enterprise*, London: NCVO.

Stewart, J. (2007) 'The mixed economy of welfare in historical context', in M. Powell (ed) *Understanding the mixed economy of welfare*, Bristol: The Policy Press, pp 26-40.

The Stationery Office (2003) *Community interest companies*, London: The Stationery Office (see also www.cicregulator.gov.uk/).

Weber, M. (1972) *The theory of social and economic organisation*, London: Collier Macmillan.

SIX

The financing of social enterprise

Wray Irwin

Introduction

Over the last 15 years there has been a growing interest in the area of social entrepreneurship, and we have seen the emergence of social enterprises as organisations that use commercial trading methods to create social value. These organisations are seen as providing solutions to social and environmental problems across the globe.

For much of that time the debate has been around defining a social enterprise in a way that enables an understanding of what makes it different from other organisational forms, so that governments can formulate policy to promote the development of more social enterprises. With much of the discussion being rooted in entrepreneurship literature, much of the thinking has been towards identifying similarities and differences between entrepreneurship and social entrepreneurship, and developing an environment in which enterprising solutions to social problems can establish and grow. It has been difficult to achieve any meaningful consensus around how this could be achieved because of a lack of consensus around the definition of a social enterprise. However, the *Social enterprise action plan: Scaling new heights*, published by the Office of the Third Sector (OTS) in 2006 proposed a number of priorities that it was felt would address the barriers to social enterprise development. These were:

- fostering a culture of social enterprise;
- ensuring that the right information and advice are available to those running social enterprises;
- enabling social enterprises to access appropriate finance;
- enabling social enterprises to work with government;
- ensuring delivery (OTS, 2006, pp 4-8).

During the consultation process for the action plan it was identified that accessing appropriate finance was a more significant barrier to starting or growing for social enterprises than commercial enterprises and needed special attention.

This chapter does not intend to address the issue of definition, but explores the issues faced by social enterprises when trying to access finance either to start or grow the organisation. These issues are addressed, however, within the OTS's definition of a social enterprise:

> A social enterprise is a business with primarily social objectives whose surpluses are principally reinvested for that purpose in the business or in the community, rather than being driven by the need to maximise profit for shareholders and owners. (OTS, 2006, p 10)

This definition identifies a social enterprise as a business first and foremost, but one that is not driven by profit alone. In fact, it is primarily driven by the need to create social value. The definition does not specify one particular legal form or organisational structure as it acknowledges that the social enterprise sector encompasses a spectrum of organisations from charities through to corporate business operations (Nicholls, 2008). In addition, it acknowledges that social enterprises borrow legal forms from all sectors of society – private, public, and civil – and very often present as hybrid structures created to address specific situations.

The diverse nature of the social enterprise sector is one of its greatest strengths, but when it comes to accessing finance it can prove to be one of the biggest barriers to starting and growing a social enterprise. Chertok et al (2008, p 46) point out that 'one of the reasons social enterprises have trouble raising money is that they do not fit neatly into either the traditional non-profit or for-profit mode'. This chapter looks at the difficulties social enterprises face when accessing funding; the range of finance options available to social enterprises, together with the positive and negative aspects of each type; and finally provides an indication of the skills that social enterpreneurs need to develop if they are to attract and manage non-traditional funding streams. Examples of useful toolkits for social entrepreneurs are given in the 'Further reading' section, see for example, Dees et al (2001).

Background

Academics, researchers, and policy makers are spending a great deal of time trying to define social entrepreneurship and identify whether it is the same or different to entrepreneurship. Chertok et al (2008, p 46) state that a social enterprise is an 'organisation or venture that advances its social mission through entrepreneurial earned income strategies'. This definition mirrors the OTS definition (OTS, 2006, p 11), which places an emphasis on business trading for social purpose.

The social and economic environment in the UK has changed considerably over the last few years. As the majority of the population has become more affluent we have become a society of consumers buying what we want when we want it, demanding lower levels of taxation so that we have more of our own money to buy what we want. This has provided a significant challenge for the delivery of public services, where patients in the National Health Service, benefit claimants, university students and parents of school children consider themselves as customers, with the expectation that they should be able to access these services when they want them rather than having to wait. Balanced against this has been the growing need to target welfare services towards those individuals who are excluded from mainstream society so that they receive the help and support they need most and in ways that provide greatest impact. All of this has placed great expectation on third sector organisations (TSOs) and in particular on social enterprises, which are seen as being able to provide the solutions to the problem of effective public service delivery.

We have also seen that the availability of grant funds for the not-for-profit organisations (NFPs), including social enterprises, has reduced due to a generally tighter funding environment and growing competition for donor and grant finance, requiring the sector to be more innovative in order to finance its activities. The need to develop trading income and other alternative funding sources has therefore become an important issue for many TSOs, and it is crucial for social enterprises.

As with all businesses, social enterprises are intended to be self-sustaining organisations that do not depend on financial donations and grants from governmental bodies, donors, or private organisations. Access to financial resources is therefore fundamental, whether that is to meet start-up costs or ongoing capital and working capital requirements.

In 2003, the Bank of England report on the financing of social enterprises identified that access to finance, in one form or another, was the main barrier to growth for the social enterprise sector (Brown and Murphy, 2003). The OTS publication *The social enterprise action plan: Scaling new heights* (OTS, 2006) recognised that little had improved in this area and made improved access to finance a priority for the plan.

However there are a number of issues that need to be addressed if improvements are to be made in accessing finance more effectively and in a way that enables growth. These can be categorised into two main areas:

- demand side
- supply side.

Demand side

Traditionally, charities, the public and the voluntary sectors have provided the spawning ground for many social enterprises and have supported their growth mainly by attracting grant funding to start the social enterprise and fund its activities. This shared heritage has passed down a mentality of grant dependency onto many of the new organisations, which gives an impression that there is an aversion to external finance within the sector. While grant finance is 'essential in creating new [social] enterprises', especially in areas where funding is scarce (Walker, 1995, cited in Smallbone et al, 2001, p 85), research has shown that many social enterprises are now adopting strategies to reduce grant dependency and move to 'contract based funding sources or to a more independent, self determining financial basis drawing ... on organisationally generated reserves and debt finance' (SQW, 2007, p 48). Concern, therefore, is not just about access to finance but also about organisational long-term sustainability.

The SQW report to the OTS on third sector access to finance (2007) identified that while a key driver for the adoption of a strategy based on reducing grant dependency has primarily been increased competition within the sector for a shrinking pool of available grants, there has also been a repositioning of grant funding – funding projects rather than core costs and investment within the organisation (SQW, 2007, p 48). This fails to build capacity within an organisation, restricting the development of a firm financial base on which to build. The result has been that many organisations experience 'mission drift' as they focus on chasing funding to survive rather than building the strategic capacity they need to deliver their social aims. Alongside this has been the ever-increasing bureaucratic burden associated with managing and monitoring grant funding, which diverts resources away from the social purpose of the organisation towards administration.

Success in implementing strategies aimed at reducing grant dependency has depended on an organisation's ability to overcome some significant barriers that restrict its ability to attract, retain and develop alternative funding. These include the organisation's legal structure, the culture of the organisation, the organisation's available asset base, and the skills sets within the organisation. Most important is the organisation's ability to generate greater levels of traded income from its activities (SQW, 2007, p 15) and be more enterprising in its approach to delivering services.

Finally, the demand for external finance is dependent on the nature of the organisation. The Bank of England identified that the demand for external finance was greater among larger social enterprises, that is, those with over 20 employees or having a £1 million turnover, which tended to have been established for a longer period of time. In addition, demand came from specific sectors such as the cooperative sector (Brown and Murphy, 2003). Increasingly, as the social enterprise sector moves to a business model centred on trading, commissioning and procurement of services rather than grants, the demand for external funding will increase, as will the need for the organisation to develop and retain business management skills in order to attract these funding sources. There is, therefore, a demand within the social enterprise sector for sources of external financial instruments other than grant funding.

Supply side

This focuses on the availability of external funding for the sector and the attitude of the finance sector to the activities of the social enterprise sector. Traditionally, the role of financial institutions has been to address market imperfections that exist within the credit markets through the pooling of deposits for lending to viable projects. Private institutions that provide credit seek to maximise profit at minimal risk to their shareholders, and in accordance with commercial criteria for making such funding available. They are more interested in the financial capability and sustainability of the borrower than the social outputs an organisation produces. Social enterprises, therefore, find that they have to prove their financial sustainability, just as any other business would, if they are to be successful in raising finance rather than present their social credentials as a reason for support. Some organisations avoid pointing out that they are social enterprises as they are 'frequently disadvantaged when they seek credit because banks frequently do not understand the nature of the [organisation] or they regard such [organisations] as inherently high risk' (Hare et al, 2006, pp 6-7).

From the lending perspective the reliance on behavioural risk scoring in making lending decisions acts as a further barrier to the supply of finance. In a 2002 report on finance for small businesses in deprived communities, the Bank of England identified the criteria on which lenders based their decisions. These were:

• credit history
• past account conduct
• willingness of client to invest their own money in the venture
• evidence of repayment capacity based on a business plan (Brown, 2002, p 36).

Such assessments and use of automated tools to predict the risk of lending to a business develop a risk profile that is compared to a generic profile of similar businesses within a sector. As social enterprises present themselves as 'normal' businesses their trading profile will present as high risk against the behavioural profile of like-for-like businesses.

On a practical level social enterprises are seen as higher risk because of the way many of them receive grant funding, and have to spend money before claiming back the grant. This presents an adverse trading trend for credit scoring purposes. In addition, the inability of social enterprises to make profit out of grant funding, thereby inhibiting their ability to generate reserves to strengthen their balance sheet, will also influence the risk assessment. At worst, such behaviours will lead them to their funding application being rejected; at best it can lead to the funding being agreed but at a higher margin than is realistic for the true level of risk.

The funding gap

Before looking at the types of funding it is important to understand what we mean by *finance*. There has been much debate over the term, as with many areas of social enterprise, and while there is no firm consensus, there is an acknowledgement that within the sector the term has a very broad meaning. For the purposes of this chapter we will, therefore, adopt the broader definition encompassing not only loans, overdrafts, equity investment and mezzanine finance, but also patient capital (described later, in the Equity section), Community Development Finance

Initiatives (CDFIs), Service Level Agreements (SLAs) and grant funding (SQW, 2007).

We will, however, group these into four main types of funding:

- **debt**, which includes **loans**, overdrafts, and other commercial lending instruments used to fund trading;
- **grants and donations**, which includes all forms of charitable donations and grant funding;
- **equity**, which includes patient and venture capital, business angels, share issues and other forms of investment capital;
- **traded income**, which includes SLAs and procurement contracts and other income generated through trading.

The application process, structure, repayment terms, interest charges among other variables differentiate these sources of funding.

The list can be expanded within each category to include services such as micro-credit, social capital venturing, and factoring and invoice discounting, with more formal larger organisations having greater capacity to access a debt and equity finance than smaller informal ones. Financial resources are critical to fund business start-up and expansion, capital projects and cash flows. Affordable credit, basic financial services and investment capital are critical to the health of communities (Benjamin et al, 2004, p 177). The features and benefits of each category of finance are described in **Figure 6.1**.

Loans

A loan is a specific amount of money that can be borrowed by a social enterprise to fund capital expansion (acquisition of assets) or to use as working capital over a specific period. Application procedures for loans are pre-defined and are assessed against a pre-set credit rating system. The borrower's credit rating, asset ownership, cash flow position, capital resources and the general operating environment are critical components of lending requirements. These aspects are summed up as the five Cs of lending: character, cash flow, collateral, capital and conditions (Green, 2005, pp 14-19).

Loans can either be secured or unsecured. Secured loans are guaranteed by assets for non-repayment and tend to be cheaper because of the reduced risk premium. A mortgage loan is an example of a secured loan as the lender holds on to the title of the house until full payment is made. When the company fails to pay, the pledged assets are taken by the lender to recover the amount of the loan owing. Non-secured loans are not guaranteed by any assets and have a higher risk premium. A credit card loan is an example of an unsecured loan.

Information required for a loan application ranges from general information (a description of the organisation, legal organisation, capital structure, location, ownership details, size and nature of business, principal activities, management

Figure 6.1: Sources and features of finance options

Source of Finance/features	Debt (loan)	Grant	Equity	Traded income
Application	Application form plus additional organisational and financial information	Grant funding proposal/application form in a format required	Offer of shares prospectus to target shareholders, or pitch to investor	Invitation to tender or proposal form submitted in appropriate format
Turnaround	Fast and in accordance with the needs of the business and lender	Fixed application times and deadlines	Company valuation process and offer prospectus. Opening and closing date of share offer, time to undertake due diligence can delay the process	Fixed application deadlines and times. For trading it is dependent on business and marketing plan implementation
Repayment	Amounts borrowed plus interest set down in agreement forms	No repayment	Dividends and bonus payouts, or exit strategy identified	Some SLAs contain claw back for non performance; however, only need to refund customers if faulty service provided
Term	Flexible – can be short, medium or long term	Fixed term – usually short to medium term	Medium to long term	Varies, dependent on the contract
Size/amount	Small to medium	Fixed amounts	Large amounts	Varies
Reporting requirements	Organisational monitoring requirements with limited reporting	Strict activity and outputs report requirements	Moderate disclosure as per shareholding/investment agreement	Minimal but in line with requirements of client
Security/collateral	Security may be required	No security required	No security required investor will want a shareholding	No security required
Risks	Assets at risk for loan repayment failure	Mission drift – shift of organisational focus to meet donor/sponsor outputs	No assets at risk. Ordinary shareholders claim residual value	Minimal risks to the organisation

structures, marketing and competitive information) to specific financial history (audited results for three years, cash flow, borrowing history references) and projections information (cash flow and business performance projections and key assumptions).

The loan lending requirements present an access barrier to informally structured social ventures that do not have credit history and cash flow viability. This explains why social ventures tend to pursue government and donor grant funding. Loans are typically sourced from banks and social enterprises have to compete for the limited resources with various organisations including well-established companies listed on the stock exchange and high growth ventures.

Grants and donations

This is one of the most traditional and familiar forms of funding for social enterprise. Government, donors, private organisations and corporate social responsibility do support the third sector through the provision of grant and donor funding. Grants and donations are usually available at particular times of the year, in limited and specified amounts and for short to medium time periods. Application is through the submission of a grant funding proposal in line with guidelines provided by the grant provider. Competition for grant funding is intensifying and therefore funding is no longer easily accessible. Grants and donations usually carry terms and conditions relating to targets and outcomes that need to be fulfilled for funding to continue. The concept of fulfilling the objectives of the funding agency, which may not be in line with the social organisation's priorities, is described as mission drift.

Equity

Equity funding is where an investor provides capital and in return gets to own a part of the business. Venture capitalists target high-growth companies from which they intend to make money through dividends and when the company gets listed on the stock exchange. A new concept of social venture capitalist is emerging to provide finance to socially and environmentally viable projects. The investors expect a return on investment and therefore seek to support profitable endeavours. Equity funding provides large sums of money for the medium to long term.

There are two main types of shares: voting and non-voting shares, commonly known as class A and class B shares, respectively. Voting shares allow the investor to participate in company decision making at board level. Shares can also be ordinary shares or preference shares with the latter not having voting rights but a guaranteed dividend before payout to any other shareholders. The organisation seeking funding is expected to write down a prospectus, which is a document that outlines the security being offered to investors and full details about the company. Issuing of shares can be private or public; the latter calls for approval by the listing authority of the stock exchange.

Over recent years we have seen the rise in social venture capital funds that are more interested in investing in the social aims of a business rather than necessarily maximising returns. The China case study (Chapter Twelve) illustrates the latter approach, where the social entrepreneurs invested in two projects focusing not purely on profit maximisation but on a social enterprise strategy that linked profit generation with clear social aims, and where value generated to the local community was also seen as important and a criterion for success.

Social venture capital funds, provided by organisations such as Adventure Capital Fund, Triodos Bank, and Philanthropy Capital, direct funds provided through the Corporate Social Responsibility budgets of investors to social enterprises and third sector organisations. The rate of return expected on such investments is much lower than for commercial propositions, with the return on the investment being deferred into the future in many cases. This relieves the social enterprise from the pressure of paying a dividend and growing at a rate determined by the investors' needs, and not those of the business. Also social venture capitalists understand the difficulty in taking a stake in a social enterprise, so will not insist on this happening, but will provide expertise to support the organisation regardless. Such support is often rewarded when the business has grown sufficiently to repay the investment at a premium. Such investment has become known as 'patient capital'.

The availability of such equity finance places a great emphasis on an organisation being able to measure its performance and in particular its social impact, 'giving a meaningful account of [their] stewardship of resources' (Patton, 2007, p 1) in order to attract investment. Increasingly a range of tools are being utilised to measure the social impact of social enterprises. The New Economics Foundation (nef) identifies over 20 such tools ranging from Quality First, 'aimed at small organisations that are run solely by volunteers' (nef, 2009, p 55), to Social Return on Investment (SROI), which provides an 'outcomes-based measurement tool that helps organisations to understand and quantify the social, environmental and economic value they are creating' (nef, 2009, p 68). Whatever method is adopted depends on the organisation and the requirements of the investors; however, all require additional management and systems to be introduced that link the financial effectiveness of an organisation to its ability to have an impact and deliver the social benefits an investor requires. It is no longer enough to do good work; an organisation needs to be able to prove that it has an impact if it wishes to access funding.

Traded income

As indicated by the OTS definition of social enterprise (OTS, 2006) there is a requirement that a social enterprise evidences some level of trading activity that contributes to the organisation's achievement of social impact. In some cases the need to fund a traded income strategy is the reason that traditional funding and equity funding is accessed. In others traded income is seen as a way of maintaining income levels when grants have been cut. In either case, the business case needs to be strong, and the implications of the adoption of a traded income strategy for the organisation, and its ability to deliver against its social mission, needs to be understood. A key consideration when exploring the adoption of a traded income strategy is to understand who the customer is, that is, who will pay for the goods and services provided.

As Dees points out, 'in an ideal world social enterprises would receive funding … only when they produce their intended social impact' (Dees, 1998, p 61) with the beneficiaries paying for the services they receive. This, of course, is very rarely possible as the impacts delivered may be for the benefit of society rather than enjoyed by the individual 'consumers' of the services provided. Services delivered for the rehabilitation of offenders, for example, provide a benefit to the individual in terms of making a life change; however, that life change has as great an impact on society in terms of reductions in crime and the potential increased economic activity of that individual. In such a case the individuals going through such a service may not value what is provided so will not pay. Alternatively, as such services are provided by social enterprises because there is a market failure preventing other providers entering the market, the beneficiaries cannot pay for what has been provided because of lack of income or because the actual price would be too prohibitive for them to afford.

This difficulty in charging beneficiaries for the services they receive leads many social enterprises to seek 'third party payers with vested interests' (Dees, 1998, p 62) to buy the services on behalf of beneficiaries. This is not an altruistic gesture, but one driven by the third parties' need to maximise the social return of the services they provide or commission and their need to find new delivery mechanisms to provide services they can no longer afford to provide. With reductions in the availability of grant funding many more third parties are looking for contracts with social enterprises, on a contracted commercial basis under SLAs or straightforward contracting of services, rather than providing grants to deliver outputs and objectives. This allows third parties, such as local authorities, to utilise procurement budgets and the procurement of service deliverers to purchase social outputs and outcomes rather than rely on specific grant funding to achieve such outputs. The relationship between the third party and the social enterprise becomes a commercial arrangement and is regulated by commercial considerations and requirements.

The benefits of such arrangements to the social enterprise can be a significant reduction in the administration costs as such contractual arrangements tend to come without the administrative burden of grants and equity reporting requirements. However, this benefit can be outweighed by the financial difficulties such arrangements can cause especially if payments are linked to output achievement and costs are incurred even though outputs may not follow. More significant is the tension that can arise between the social enterprise's social mission and the vested interests of the payer; in particular how closely the payer shares the social mission of the social enterprise. If there is any possibility that the social enterprise's mission is incompatible or divergent from the interests of the player, there are major risks that the social enterprise will suffer from mission drift or end up adopting the interests of the payer just to ensure it can win and retain contracts.

Traded income is not therefore the panacea to reductions in traditional funding streams, as the adoption of a traded income startegy sometimes requires other forms of finance to be obtained in order to be successful. Traded income strategies bring new and more complex challenges to social enterprises and their managers that require clear strategies and business management to ensure that the enterprise activities deliver the intended social impact and do not undermine the stability, both financially and organisationally, of the social enterprise.

Conclusion

There is now a range of finance options available to social enterprises and the wider third sector. Organisations cannot rely solely on grant funding as their only source of income, and are increasingly looking to traded income models to secure sustainability. While, historically, traditional sources of external finance have not been accessible to the third sector, developments in financial instruments have increased the supply of available finance.

However, these more commercial types of funding, coupled with an increasingly competitive grant environment require social enterprises to approach providers of finance in a more professional and business-like manner. Providers of finance need to see that an organisation is properly managed, has vision, and the right skills in order to deliver effectively and repay any finance obtained. This places a greater emphasis on skills such as business planning, financial management, budgeting, and the production of timely and accurate management information. It requires those running social enterprises to emphasise the business capacity of the organisation to instil confidence in those they approach for financial support. The days when organisations received finance just because they 'did good work' are a thing of the past.

References

Benjamin, L., Rubin, J.S. and Zielenbach, S. (2004) 'Community development financial institutions: current issues and future prospects', *Journal of Urban Affairs*, vol 26, issue 2, pp 177-95.

Brown, H. (2002) *Finance for small businesses – a ninth report*, London: Bank of England (www.bankofengland.co.uk/publications/financeforsmallfirms/fin4sm09.pdf).

Brown, H. and Murphy, E. (2003) *The financing of social enterprises: A special report by the Bank of England*, London: Bank of England (www.bankofengland.co.uk/publications/financeforsmallfirms/financing_social_enterprise_report.pdf).

Chertok, M., Hamaoui, J. and Jamison, E. (2008) 'The funding gap', *Stanford Social Innovation Review*, Spring 2008.

Dees, J. G. (1998) 'Enterprising nonprofits', *Harvard Business Review*, January/February, pp 55–100.

Green, Charles H. (2005) *The SBA loan book: Get a small business loan – even with poor credit, weak collateral, and no experience* (2nd edn), Avon, MA: Adams Media.

Hare, P., Jones, D. and Blackledge, G. (2006) *Understanding social enterprise and its financing: Case study of the child-care sector in Scotland*, Edinburgh: Lloyds TSB.

nef (New Economics Foundation) (2009) *Tools for you: Approaches to proving and improving for charities voluntary sector organisations and social enterprise* (2nd edn), (www.neweconomics.org/sites/neweconomics.org/files/Tools_for_You_1.pdf).

Nicholls, A. (2008) *Social entrepreneurship: New models of sustainable social change*, Oxford: Oxford University Press.

OTS (The Office for the Third Sector) (2006) *The social enterprise action plan: Scaling new heights*, London: Cabinet Office.

Patton, R. (2007) *Managing and measuring social enterprise*, London: Sage Publications.

Smallbone, D., Evans, M., Ekanem, I., and Butters, S. (2001) *Researching social enterprise*, London: Centre for Enterprise and Economic Development Research, Middlesex University.

SQW (2007) *Research on third sector access to finance: Report to the Office of the Third Sector*, London: Cabinet Office (www.cabinetoffice.gov.uk/third_sector/news/news_stories/070618_finance_access.aspx),(also available at www.sqw.co.uk/file_download/128).

Further reading

Dees, J. G., Emerson, J. and Economy, P. (2001) *Enterprising non-profits: A toolkit for social entrepreneurs*, New York: John Wiley & Sons.

Dees, J. G., Emerson, J. and Economy, P. (2002) *Strategic tools for social entrepreneurs: Enhancing the performance of your enterprising nonprofit*, New York: John Wiley & Sons.

Lewis, H. (2009) *Bids, tenders, and proposals: Winning business through best practice* (3rd edn), London: Kogan Page.

nef (New Economics Foundation) (2005) *Credit where it's due: Access to loan finance for social enterprises in South West England*, Exeter: RISE.

Quick, J. and New, C. (2000) *Grant winner's toolkit: Project management and evaluation*, New York: John Wiley & Sons.

Pearce, J. (2003) *Social enterprise in anytown*, London: Calouste Gulbenkian Foundation.

Website resources

Social Enterprise Coalition: www.socialenterprise.org.uk/
Social Return on Investment – European network: www.sroi-europe.org/

SEVEN

Financial planning for social enterprises

Andrew Ferguson

Introduction

Very few people become social entrepreneurs with the ambition of managing money, although, as earlier chapters have made clear, the generation of funds to assure sustainability and growth is one of the defining features of the social enterprise. While money is not the end objective of a social enterprise it is always worth bearing in mind that nothing very much can happen without it and therefore its careful management is essential to securing the wider objectives of the enterprise. This chapter looks at how the financial elements of a social enterprise are integrated into its business plan and also at some of the basic techniques managers can use to check on the financial health of the enterprise once it is up and running.

The financial components this chapter will look at are: the income forecast, the income statement and the cash flow forecast. There are many other elements to managing finances than these three tools; however, without an understanding of these three it is unlikely that a social enterprise will get past the stage of simply being a 'good idea'.

It is good to plan

Business plans are commonly associated with commercial start-ups where they are often used to secure external funds by demonstrating the viability and ultimate success of the enterprise. Social enterprises need business plans too. Putting together a plan for a social enterprise could be said to be more complex than the same process for a commercial venture. A social enterprise business plan not only needs to consider the same customer and marketing issues as its commercial equivalent but it must also demonstrate a genuine, measurable social benefit to its activities. Both commercial and social enterprise business plans conclude with a forecast of the financial health of the venture, giving an indication of its potential viability. However, as the US case study (Chapter Eleven) shows, social entrepreneurs need to maintain the mission and purpose of the organisation while generating profits.

The process of setting out the objectives of the social enterprise alongside its strategy for delivering them and generating the resources to do so has tremendous value for those involved. As well as helping to clarify thought, a plan can also be seen as a paper 'model' of the enterprise. Needless to say, if the enterprise does not work on paper it is highly unlikely that it will work in reality. Plans developed by prospective management teams can also ensure a common understanding of what is being attempted. A failure to agree on a single vision for the enterprise is better discovered at the planning stage rather than once actual time and resources are committed. So it is good to make plans, even if reality inevitably disrupts them.

Money is often the last element to be addressed in a business plan. This is because the financial profile of the social enterprise is entirely dependent on what it is trying to achieve and the strategy it has for doing this. The social entrepreneur has hopefully identified what the enterprise actually does, who will want its services and, importantly, who will pay for them and why. Payment could be coming from a variety of sources ranging from grants and donations through to commercial transactions, although as we are discussing social enterprises rather than charities, we must assume that a significant proportion of income will be generated by the enterprise itself delivering something of financial value to a customer rather than appealing to the generosity of a donor.

With these 'market' assumptions in place the social entrepreneur can start the process of building up a financial picture of the enterprise. The spreadsheet is the essential tool for financial forecasting. A number of websites offer downloadable financial formats for these purposes and many banks will provide template software free of charge. Organisations such as Business Link also offer help to get financial forecasts into commonly accepted formats that will make sense to banks and other potential funders.

By setting up a spreadsheet 'book' it is possible to get information to read across all the individual forecasts, from income through to cash flow. This considerably reduces the amount of inputting time required but, more importantly, allows the implications of variations in forecasting assumptions to be immediately calculated. The process of considering the financial implications of how major 'what ifs' will impact on a business is known as sensitivity analysis.

Of course, all business plans are built up on a number of assumptions and for a plan to show the financial implications of every single one would mean that the social entrepreneur would never actually get round to starting operations. Much better is for the author(s) of the business plan to show that they have identified the crucial determinants of the success or otherwise of the enterprise and demonstrate only a limited number of fundamentally important and well-explained scenarios in their financial forecasts. For example, if the enterprise is not energy intensive then presenting a sensitivity analysis based on rises/falls in energy prices is of little value. However, if high sales are felt to be largely dependent on getting into the marketplace before any other organisation then a 'what if we get there second?' analysis becomes very important.

Income forecast

In a commercial business the income forecast might also be termed a 'sales forecast'. As we saw in the previous chapter, 'trading' is becoming a significantly important part of income generation for many social enterprises, and in the UK case study (Chapter Ten) you can see clearly how commercial considerations are a significant factor for a successful social entrepreneur. However, as we have already established, the concept of 'sales' may or may not apply in the context of all social enterprises and it is sometimes prudent to separate out income generated by the enterprise's own operations from that associated with donations to discover the true viability of the 'business' element of the enterprise. What will definitely apply is the need to identify when revenue-generating activity will take place and what revenue it will produce. An income forecast will therefore be a spreadsheet that shows a time period – commonly 12 to 24 months – on the horizontal axis and identifies the individual sources of income that are anticipated to come to the enterprise over that period on the vertical axis. Analysis of the income forecast will allow the social entrepreneur to:

1. calculate how the enterprise's marketing strategy will generate income /sales – how many and over what time frame;
2. generate an anticipated amount of revenue in that period, drawing from the enterprise's pricing strategy;
3. determine the costs of funding the activity required to meet the income forecast and generate a figure for the cost of delivery;
4. create a business plan that then presents a gross profit (income less costs).

Forecasting income depends on a whole series of assumptions. These might include macro-economic issues, such as interest rates, unpredictable features such as the weather, or be relevant only to the individual enterprises, such as securing one particular contract. A realistic assumption, informed by a good knowledge of the market the enterprise serves, is required, but at the end of the day it remains an estimate – a guess, albeit an informed one. The case study from India (Chapter Thirteen) shows the difficulties social enterprises can face with price; in this study the crash in the global price of tea led to the need to develop a new pricing strategy.

In forecasting income there is a tremendous temptation for social entrepreneurs to be overly optimistic both in terms of the amount of income likely to come to the enterprise but also the speed at which this will be realised. This optimism is understandable as they are likely to be individuals with a passion and enthusiasm for what they are offering, but can also be damaging for new enterprise. For example, it is unlikely that a new enterprise can go from a standing start to near optimal sales in a matter of weeks. It will take time for sales staff to contact potential customers, or for advertising to reach its intended target audience. A common error for social enterprises is to underestimate the time taken to get through formal procurement procedures, such as those commonly used by the public sector, where contracts to deliver services are commonly offered up for competitive tender, a process that can take many months and involve considerable work, none of which anyone pays for. Once a competitive proposal is identified as 'the best' it can take months to actually negotiate contracts for delivery, again with no one paying for the time invested. Building in development time into any planning process is crucial for the success of any organisation; however, this developmental phase is unlikely to contribute in the short term to income generation.

It is also important to be aware of the delivery capacity of the enterprise when forecasting income based on paid activity. If the enterprise does secure revenue-generating business how much of its capacity will be absorbed by undertaking the delivery process? Does this absorbed capacity mean that other activities cannot be undertaken, even if they were potentially more valuable? For a small social enterprise capacity can be a real issue (see the example in **Box 7.1**).

Box 7.1: Retail therapy

This potential social enterprise was proposed by a former nurse with considerable experience of working in homes for older people. The plan was to provide residents with a service that enabled them to discuss their footwear needs with a trained shoe fitter, who could then order and deliver directly into the home with no need for the resident to undertake the hassle of a shopping trip. As the service would be one-to-one there would also be the opportunity for the customer to have a chat as well.

Once forecasting calculations were made it was found that an estimate of half an hour per client – quite a short duration for a service based on social interaction – plus travel time for the one shoe fitter meant that even working six days a week for eight hours per day could not generate a sufficient volume of sales to reach the income levels needed to sustain the service. In short, the service absorbed more capacity than it generated revenue.

The income forecast also depends on the social entrepreneur understanding what price to charge for the product or service being offered. Developing a pricing strategy is an issue potentially worthy of a chapter of its own but some general observations can be made. First, being a social enterprise does not necessarily mean that prices need to be cheaper than commercial alternatives. Indeed consumers have time and again demonstrated their willingness to pay extra for products and services that offer an ethical or social dimension – up to a point. The point when a willingness to pay for the 'right thing' gives way to the need to save money is something that social entrepreneurs must judge, using their knowledge of the market.

The second significant observation may appear obvious but can catch out those unfamiliar with commercial operations; do not charge less for a product or service than it costs you to deliver it. Here it is important to account for all the expenses that the enterprise faces but are not directly related to the product or service; for example, all that time you put into writing the competitive tender documents, the time spent completing all the administration for the enterprise, and the power, heat and light used simply by running an office. Get this wrong and the harder the enterprise works the more money it will lose (see **Box 7.2**).

Box 7.2: Freda Fit

This one-woman enterprise offered primary-aged children after-school exercise and health awareness classes. To make these classes attractive the social entrepreneur decided to make them free to the beneficiaries and to look for funding from charitable and public funds. Perhaps unsurprisingly, free after-school childcare proved very popular with both parents and schools, making the entrepreneur extremely busy – too busy in fact to put the research and time into winning the external funds to make the programme sustainable. Exhausted and without funds the social entrepreneur decided to wind up the enterprise, reflecting afterwards that charging the beneficiaries a modest amount from the outset would have helped reduce the dependence on external sources of funding and would have been affordable to many of those using the service.

A completed income forecast therefore gives an estimate of when income-generating activities will take place and what income those activities will attract. Importantly, it does not necessarily show when the cash comes into the enterprise, which is the function of the cash flow forecast.

Income statement

The common term for this financial planning tool is the profit and loss account. Social enterprises sometimes have difficulty with the word 'profit' and substitute the word surplus instead, although the end results are the same. No independent organisation can develop or grow without making a profit at some stage and although social enterprises are generally concerned to reinvest their profits in the activities of the enterprise, rather than enriching the social entrepreneur on a personal level, these profits need to be generated in the first place. The income statement is a prediction based on the income forecast of whether a profit will be made within the same time frame.

To find the profit of an enterprise means understanding and being able to detail not only its income but also its costs. Costs come in all shapes and sizes and can be predicted, and subsequently controlled, by the social entrepreneur with a far greater degree of precision than income. A spreadsheet of the enterprise's predicted costs should form part of the ongoing financial forecast frequently revisited by its managers.

The process of generating gross revenue from operations, as shown in the income forecast, will generally cost an enterprise money, sometimes known as the 'cost of sales'. As well as knowing what the market will pay for a product or service, social entrepreneurs also need to have a good grasp of how much it will cost them to produce a unit of it. This is true of a single saleable item, an hour of consultancy advice or a tonne of compost.

Some of the costs of getting the product or service to the customer are 'direct'. These can, very simply, be divided into two broad groups:

- fixed costs – those which will not vary whether the enterprise is extremely busy or stands idle, such as rent on premises;
- variable costs – those that will vary with the levels of activity undertaken, such as raw materials, distribution costs.

However, there are other costs which are 'indirect,' sometimes known as operating costs, which also need to be accounted for. These costs can include:

- *Depreciation.* This is incurred when buying a capital item, that is, a significant item with a productive life of more than 12 months, such as a vehicle for distribution purposes. Showing the full cost of this item on the income statement in year one of the enterprise's activities would make it look very unhealthy, yet in year two there would be a massive reduction in costs. Neither position would be truly representative of the actual performance of the enterprise as a business. Depreciation smoothes this process by writing off the cost of the item over its anticipated working life to give a clearer impression of how the business is really operating. For example, an item worth £50,000 with an anticipated useful life of five years is shown in each year's income statement as £10,000 worth of depreciation.
- *Employee costs.* In smaller enterprises staff will try to carry out every function of the business, from directly producing the product/service to marketing and sales. All staff activities should be contributing to the running of the business and are therefore profit and loss costs. Although some social enterprises rely on volunteers to carry out some of their activities, those which are capable of development and growth generally require full-time professional, paid-for, staff.
- *Marketing and promotion.* It is often quite difficult to separate out the 'bit' of marketing that leads directly to a sale. Marketing is often a complex mix of direct promotion and raising awareness. Unfortunately all of it tends to cost something, even if it is only time that could have been spent elsewhere.

These are operating costs and offer the entrepreneur a degree of flexibility in planning an enterprise. Deciding how much should be spent on promotion and marketing and how much on employees are questions of fine judgment and it is usually worth taking the views of an experienced adviser or mentor into consideration when planning to answer them.

Fixed costs can mount up very quickly as an enterprise expands and it is sometimes difficult to reduce them once they become integrated into day-to-day operations. This is particularly true of paid staff, who may even be personal friends.

Caution in building up the fixed cost base of an enterprise is always advisable and social entrepreneurs should think very hard about accepting contracts that oblige them to take on fixed costs (see **Box 7.3**).

This enterprise provides environmental education to the public. It was funded by a combination of grants and sales of services such as advice and training courses. It was successful in bidding for additional funds to run further services, and over time the operation grew from a staff base of just two up to eight, and attracted more volunteers, visitors and customers to the centre. On reviewing the income forecast, the management team realised that the income generated to fund the new activity did not cover full operating costs relating to human resources processes for staff, increased office costs and growing wear and tear on the centre caused by more people using the site. This left the management team in the position of having to revise future income projections, consider cutting costs and ensure that future business plans took into account the hidden costs behind delivering services.

Income less costs equals profit, or surplus if that is how you would prefer to think of it. Incidentally, the word 'profit' can appear in a number of guises. We have already seen 'gross profit', which is income less the cost of sales, and 'operating profit', which is gross profit less operating costs. However, there is also 'operating profit with contingency'; adding back any unspent contingency gives 'actual operating profit'; ignoring taxation gives 'profit before taxation' and finally taking out taxation and any interest payable gives 'net profit available for appropriation'. This is the real bottom line that will generally go back into the enterprise.

Cash flow forecast

It is sometimes said that accountants produce profits while businesses produce cash. It is certainly true that a business goes bust when it has not got the cash to pay its creditors, not necessarily when it makes an accounting loss. Cash flow is therefore vital to the survival and success of any business and is, in many ways, a better indicator of viability than the income statement. While capital expenditure is spread over the depreciation life of the equipment, the impact of such a purchase on the enterprise's cash flow is immediate and potentially fatal if the funds are not there to meet the cost. Forecasting cash flow is also the means by which the entrepreneur can gauge how much investment is needed to get the enterprise up and running.

A cash flow forecast spreadsheet looks very similar to the income forecast but for the crucial difference that the figures show real money entering and leaving the enterprise's bank account as and when it is anticipated to actually do so. For example, every month on the first day of the month cash for the rent of premises will leave the enterprise. Along with staff wages and other running expenses, cash is needed to meet bills regardless of the highly profitable contract the enterprise is engaged in but, crucially, has not been paid for yet. Many social entrepreneurs with career backgrounds in the public sector often remark on the shock the relentless struggle cash flow causes. Whereas many public sector organisations are proficient at working within budgets, cash flow is about having ready cash at hand exactly when needed and having little or no capacity to go into the 'red' on a consistent basis. To repeat the phrase above – a business goes bust when it has not got the cash to pay its creditors.

Table 7.1 and **Table 7.2** illustrate the difference between forecasting income and forecasting cash flow. **Table 7.1** shows the income implications of taking on a particular contract.

Table 7.1: Income forecast

	January	February	March	April	May
Income	£1,000	£2,000	£2,500	£3,500	£5,000
Less: variable costs	£500	£1,200	£1,500	£2,000	£2,500
Less: fixed costs	£1,000	£1,000	£1,000	£1,000	£1,000
Net surplus	−£500	−£200	£0	£500	£1,500
Cumulative surplus	−£500	−£700	−£700	−£200	£1,300

The contract generates a surplus, albeit after a few months, and may therefore seem attractive to the enterprise. **Table 7.2** forecasts the cash implications of the same contract and makes a number of realistic assumptions about the movement of real money during the initial few months of delivery. These assumptions are that the cash income will be paid 60 days after delivery of the service, that variable costs can be paid 30 days after being incurred and fixed costs will have to be paid at the same time each month.

Table 7.2: Cash flow forecast

	January	February	March	April	May
Income	£0	£0	£1,000	£2,000	£2,500
Less: variable costs	£0	£500	£1,200	£1,500	£2,000
Less: fixed costs	£1,000	£1,000	£1,000	£1,000	£1,000
Net surplus	−£1,000	−£1,500	−£1,200	−£500	−£500
Cumulative surplus	−£1,000	−£2,500	−£3,700	−£4,200	−£4,700

The contract is still profitable, but will need a significant overdraft, or access to reserve funds, to actually deliver it. Provided that the management of the enterprise, and potentially their bank, are expecting this then the contract may well be worth picking up. If they were not expecting to carry a significant overdraft and credit cannot be obtained then the contract is inviting the enterprise to go bust.

Cash flow is derived from the income forecast combined with a clear understanding of the likely costs the enterprise will incur in order to earn that income. It also depends on understanding how purchasing and sales are handled in the market in which the enterprise operates. For example, an enterprise that simply buys and sells Fairtrade products from around the world, rather than manufacturing them, will need to understand what credit terms it can obtain from its suppliers and what credit terms it can safely offer its customers. Can customers be expected to pay 'up front' for the products or by using staged payments? What form of payment terms do competitors offer and do these make them more attractive? A profitable contract can bankrupt a business if payment arrives too late to help pay for the costs of delivering it.

Box 7.4 gives an example of how important it is to manage cash flow.

Box 7.4: Re-Oil

Re-Oil is a social enterprise that recycles catering and agricultural oils for other uses. Every month its management team meet and review the cash flow forecast asking the question 'If we bring in only the money we are 100% guaranteed to receive how long will our enterprise survive on the cash we have available?' This is a sobering question and very often the answer is only a couple of months. However, it also brings into focus the need to manage cash and secure contracts that pay reliably and promptly.

There are a number of things that social entrepreneurs can do to help manage cash flow. An obvious one is to collect the money owed to the enterprise promptly and efficiently and, if at all possible, get payment in advance of delivering the product or service. The converse is also true: attempting to lengthen the credit terms available to the enterprise rather than simply paying bills as soon as they are received also helps to keep cash to hand. Checking out potential customers before offering credit should be systematically and regularly carried out, working only with those with a reliable track record of payment.

One of the more reliable payers for the services offered by social enterprises is the public sector. Unfortunately, although the sector is reliable it can also be very slow and bureaucratic in the process of making its payments. It can also be inflexible in its dealings with suppliers, no matter how socially valuable the goods and services or how warm the individual relationships involved. A cash flow forecast should account for the problems of a typical waiting period and be aware of the risk of having an invoice rejected, not because the product or service supplied was poor, but because the accompanying paperwork was not exactly as specified by the purchaser's accounts department.

Other techniques to keep cash in the enterprise include leasing rather than buying major purchases and keeping stocks of goods or raw materials to the minimum needed to operate on. Cash is the life blood of any enterprise and it must never be taken for granted.

Managing financial risk

According to Howard Stevenson of the Harvard Business School one of the defining features of an entrepreneur is the 'pursuit of opportunity without regard to resources currently controlled' (Stevenson, 1999). This means that, unlike an administrative manager controlling a fixed budget, social entrepreneurs do not allow available funds to constrain their thinking. Instead they accept that bringing in new resources is part of the process of developing an opportunity. This means that risk is generally a constant feature of any entrepreneurial venture, social or otherwise and is managed as such by the entrepreneur. As stated in the introduction, the US case study (Chapter Eleven) explores this trait and distinguishes between reckless risk takers and successful entrepreneurs who 'manage risk'. Common financial risks can be identified and should be constantly managed. Some of these are:

- *Overestimating income.* Without optimism an enterprise might never get started but it is also important to have access to someone with a sober and realistic view of the likelihood of bringing in the money anticipated so that the enterprise does not build up costs and commitments to a scale that cannot be met should income be less than expected.
- *Relying on one source of income.* Tempting though it is to work exclusively with one reliable and generous customer it is always a risk to have all the eggs in one basket (see example in **Box 7.5**). The more diverse the sources of income the greater the chances the enterprise has of surviving a sudden shift in customer needs.
- *Losing track of costs.* Fixed costs in particular can be relentlessly draining for any enterprise and can accumulate quickly if allowed to. Keeping costs low is as important as winning income if a consistent surplus is to be made and it is vital that the cost implications of all activities are considered carefully before committing the enterprise to them.
- *Running out of cash.* Forecasting and closely monitoring cash flow is an essential management task that can never be neglected. No money, no social enterprise.

Box 7.5: Skill Builder

Skill Builder was a social enterprise that provided work experience and training in the building trades for individuals from disadvantaged backgrounds. On set-up it was supported by the local city council which supplied it with relatively generous contracts to build school extensions and other public facilities. After three years the enterprise was employing over 90 trainees at any one time and making a reasonable surplus, which was reinvested in equipment. Unfortunately, the city council remained its only customer. With a change in council officers the formerly close relationship ended and contracts quickly dried up. With regular and heavy cash requirements Skill Builder simply did not have the time to search out new customers before going bust.

Conclusion

Money is only a tool to achieving the ends of the social enterprise, but it is a vital one. Social entrepreneurs need to ensure that they have timely and accurate financial information to hand at all times if they are to manage their activities effectively. Although they are rarely constrained by the resources immediately to hand they are also fully aware of those they do have. This chapter has provided a basic description of the strategies required to keep control of the financial aspects of a social enterprise.

Reference
Stevenson, H. (1999) *The entrepreneurial venture*, Boston MA: Harvard Business School Press.

EIGHT

The challenges and risks of innovation in social entrepreneurship

Tim Curtis

Introduction

Innovation is key for social enterprises. It is deemed to be the feature that distinguishes them most clearly from charities. Indeed, the Social Enterprise Coalition, in its response to the Department for Innovation, Universities and Skills Science, and Innovation Strategy Consultation claimed that social enterprise is an inherently innovative business model. Innovation was the subject of a series of Office of the Third Sector position papers by Leadbeater (2007), Nicholls, A. (2007), Nicholls, J. (2007), Aiken (2007) and Westall (2007). The National Endowment for Science and Technology (Parker, 2009) and the Young Foundation (Mulgan, et al, 2007) have also engaged in this field with significant reviews of the literature and exhortations to all sectors of society to realise the (implicit) value of innovation to society. Further, '... not to innovate is to die' according to Christopher Freeman (1997, p 266) in his famous study of economics of innovation.

Innovation has been connected to macro-economics by what Joseph Schumpeter calls waves of destructive (and presumably constructive) economic development, whereas later work explored how firms behave differently and manage this difference in the search for competitive advantage (Woodward 1965). Trott points out that many of the early studies treat innovation as an artefact that is somehow detached from knowledge and skills and not embedded within the know-how of the organisation (Trott, 2002), which leads to a simplified understanding and a sense in which innovation can be achieved, purchased or implemented by leadership will. This tendency is also identifiable in the third sector.

Entrepreneurship and innovation are also closely associated with uncontrollable mavericks (Taylor and Labarre, 2006) or deviant (non-conformist) personality traits (Vries, 1977). Other authors have focused on innovation in the public sector (Newman et al, 2001; Mulgan and Albury, 2003; Albury, 2005), but few have explicitly considered innovation in social enterprises, except by separating social enterprises as organisations from social entrepreneurship as a process of innovation (Leadbeater, 2007). By separating the enterprise from the entrepreneur, Leadbeater allows for the consideration of innovation as an individual behaviour rather than an organisational process – such that innovation is promoted heroically by the talented individuals and only restrained by personal ethics rather than governance. Fewer authors have explicitly considered the ethics of innovation (Glor, 2003; Hanekamp, 2007; Fuglsang and Mattsson, 2009). Whereas in the private sector innovation can often be an end in itself, for Hartley innovation in public services is justifiable only where it increases public value in the quality, efficiency or fitness for purpose of governance or services (Hartley, 2005). For others, public sector innovation becomes necessary to keep pace with, in the words of Will Baumol, 'the free market innovation machine' (Baumol, 2002. p xiii).

This chapter discusses three aspects of the challenge of innovation in social enterprise. Firstly, innovation is conceptualised and its ethics are explored to set the scene for considering its practical application. Innovation is not ethically neutral, and innovation can lead to bad decisions or real harm to people and in communities. Therefore, the ethical dimension of innovation needs to be established. Having developed a sense of the ethics of innovation, systems skills required to analyse a situation are introduced, drawing on soft systems theory and an understanding of 'wicked issues'. Finally, the chapter explores some of the issues of implementing innovation, seeking to avoid a command and control approach to innovation and instead promoting a mind-set or cultural approach to innovation in the organisation. The chapter concludes with a summary of the sorts of actions that a social enterprise manager or leader may consider in promoting ethically infused innovation within social enterprises.

Innovation brings change and risk that can be in conflict with the public service principles of consistency, equity, and accountability. And so the question arises – how can a social enterprise be innovative without harming these principles?

The question poses some important differences between public and private sector innovation. Innovation in the latter is driven primarily by competitive advantage – this tends to restrict the sharing of good practice to strategic partners. By contrast, the drivers for social enterprises are to achieve widespread improvements in governance and service delivery, including efficiencies, in order to increase public value (Moore, 1995). The key to unpicking these differences is for the social entrepreneur to understand what, in society, will change through the social enterprise activity, and how that change will occur. This means going beyond the assumption that adopting a given legal structure (such as a company limited by guarantee or cooperative) will result in a certain social change.

Conceptualising innovation and its ethics

A convenient definition of innovation from an organisational perspective is given by Luecke and Katz, who wrote:

> Innovation... is generally understood as the introduction of a new thing or method .... Innovation is the embodiment, combination, or

synthesis of knowledge in original, relevant, valued new products, processes, or services. (2003, pp 2, 11)

Innovation as an organisational skill

Innovation is a personal skill, but one that is exercised within an organisational context. There is increasing literature on developing personal thinking and creativity skills (De Bono, 1968; Henry, 2001), but these are aimed at developing individual thinking processes or aimed at leadership style strategy development. On the other hand, management texts (Tidd et al, 2005; Lowe and Marriott, 2007) focus primarily on the management of innovation in contexts where innovation and change are expected and encouraged. More difficult is the process of developing innovative activities in a wider organisational context where innovation is not recognised, expected or (in the case of circumstances where experiments may result in real harm) considered inappropriate or risky. The challenge is to develop an expectation of, and processes that support, innovation within a social context, where the innovation is not a result of individualised creativity undertaken in secret activities, off-grid, or below the radar of the wider governance of the organisation.

The literature seems clear that innovation is not the same as invention because innovation requires the application of an invention to a use or good, product or service (Fagerberg, 2004). In the same style it is also possible to assert that innovation is not continuous improvement as its effects are not new to the organisation, nor large enough, general enough and durable enough to appreciably affect the operations or character of the organisation (Moore et al, 1997 p 276). Hartley (2005) draws together a number of sources to provide a typology of innovation in the provision of public services:

- **Product innovation** – new products. *Example*: Huetility Colourblind Simulator, which accurately models the different types of colour-blindness, letting a person with normal colour vision see the world through the eyes of a person with colour-blindness.
- **Service innovation** – new ways in which services are provided to users. *Example*: Awareness is a DVD presentation and training package intended for agencies within the Criminal Justice System. It will show victims' views and how their procedures can affect families of murder victims.
- **Process innovation** – new ways in which organisational processes are designed. *Example*: The Phone Co-op, which is a user-owned telecommunications company, or Nene Commissioning, which manages a budget of £275 million for 61 health practices in the East Midlands in the UK.
- **Position innovation** – new contexts or users. *Example*: Palm Cove provides supported accommodation to destitute asylum seekers being supported by social services where there is a legal obligation to provide support and accommodation

in response to unexpected health issues such as cancer, HIV, kidney failure, pregnancy, child related issues etc.

- **Strategic innovation** – new goals or purposes of the organisation. *Example*: Ealing Community Transport (ECT) was originally established in 1979 to provide transport for older and disabled people in Ealing. Over the years, ECT has become an award-winning and highly successful community transport organisation.
- **Governance innovation** – new forms of citizen engagement, and democratic institutions. *Example*: The governing council for Mondragón Corporation (based in Spain) is the 650-member Cooperative Congress, for which delegates are elected from across the individual cooperatives. The annual general assembly elects a governing council which has day-to-day management responsibility and appoints senior staff. For each individual business, there is also a workplace council, the elected president of which assists the manager with the running of the business on behalf of the workers.
- **Rhetorical innovation** – new language and new concepts. *Example*: Wikipedia is a free, web-based multilingual encyclopaedia project supported by the non-profit Wikimedia Foundation.

Rather than defining innovation in relation to its outcomes, innovation also needs to be considered in terms of its input – the skills and the contexts within which the skills are exercised.

The ethics of social change in entrepreneurship

Social enterprise texts have often focused on describing the organisational (and legal) forms of the enterprise, assuming that the legal form guarantees the social impact or social innovation. Instead, social enterprises should be categorised according to the mode of social change. The underlying assumptions of the key entrepreneurs involved in the development of the business concept have an important influence on the nature of the business pursued and the organisational strategies adopted.

A good example is the case of Greyston Bakery, which supplies cookies to Ben & Jerry's Inc. Putting aside the ambiguities around Ben & Jerry's corporate social responsibility (Bryan et al, 1998), the mission statement of Greyston Bakery is 'We don't hire people to bake brownies; we bake brownies to hire people'. This is clearly a different model to a mainstream bakery, which might be said to employ people (who happen to make cookies) to create personal wealth or return on investment for shareholders. Greyston just happens to be making cookies – they could equally be making and selling other products. Instead, Greyston exists to employ people. Indeed, if they chose to use new equipment to reduce the cost of the wages and thereby make cheaper cookies, they would be drifting from their core mission of job creation. Reducing their employee count while increasing production would not be a strategy that Greyston could adopt. But on the same statement of principles on their website, Greyston commits: 'The bakery will automate its production whenever such changes are fiscally appropriate' (Anon, 2009a) In other words, Greyston envisages the possibility of reducing its employment costs through automation, and thereby reducing the number of people it employs per cookie made.

Notwithstanding this problem, there is also a limitation with respect to Greyston's theory of social change. Their concept of a just society is predicated on employment. Their underlying assumption is that being employed is a good way out of social exclusion for the people of Southwest Yonkers, New York, where they operate. Another social enterprise might think that being educated is the most important issue (see Chapter Ten) and implement a training or education programme, or another might think that being able to travel to where the jobs are is more equitable, and thereby implement a transport scheme.

So, the social issue, and how it is framed, has a fundamental influence on the type of entrepreneurial opportunity that is considered. Innovation in developing the solution, in this respect, lies in the way in which a problem is conceptualised in the first place.

There are three dimensions of the social enterprise that directly affect the entrepreneurial orientations of the organisation as it develops and grows. These three dimensions both promote and limit innovation providing a context within which the innovation occurs. In developing a social enterprise, choices regarding the **model of social change employed**, the **marketplace** in which the organisation operates and the **organisational strategy** it adopts provide an inescapable infrastructure within which the organisation will operate. Its future ability to innovate and remain innovative depends on the choices made in these three aspects.

Ethics in the choice of marketplace

There are three contexts within which a social enterprise might appear, whereas the mainstream business literature assumes two. For mainstream business, a new venture occurs as an entirely new organisation or in the context of an existing organisation (intrapreneurship). In the social enterprise world, a social entrepreneur might emerge from an existing charity or civil society organisation; from the activity of government (local authority or governmental agency such as the NHS); or (perhaps less frequently) as a spin-in from the private sector, where an existing private sector entrepreneur or employee leaves the sector to establish his or her own socially oriented business. This third group also overlaps with the 'lifestyle entrepreneurship' (Schine, 2003) subculture of 'one person initiatives' and 'alternative movement adherents' seeking to make a living outside corporate structures. There is some overlap between these enterprises and social enterprises, but one might consider the extent to which the social enterprise grows and serves a wider circle of concern than the individual and/or family.

The different cultural contexts from which social entrepreneurs emerge have an effect on the type of marketplace that the enterprise enters, the organisational options chosen and the strategic cultures adopted. While Leiter (2005), investigating Australian non-profits, found no robust evidence of social enterprises copying each other's practices within a sector, others (Sellers, 2003) have noted the pressure on organisations working with the public sector to adopt public sector practices and norms. This occurs, for example, when a local authority in the UK seeks to spin-off a non-essential function out into a social enterprise. Not only will employment conditions, such as final salary pensions, have to be established in the new enterprise (under the Transfer of Undertakings [Protection of Employment] Regulations), but even the way in which a board is run will reflect the sponsorship of the public sector (Curtis, 2004). Stinchcombe (1965) identified that new organisations suffer from an inherent 'liability of newness' and, in order to ensure their legitimacy, the new organisation adopts clearly defined templates from peers and stakeholders.

A social enterprise emerging from an existing charity will share some of its organisational characteristics with the parent, but more importantly, the marketplace within which it operates will often be related to the charitable objectives of the charity. Likewise, social enterprises emerging from the public sector will predominantly provide services and products that are closely related to policy objectives. Often, grant funding is available to third sector organisations that are not otherwise available to statutory bodies, and the statutory body is tempted to spin-out a separate social enterprise to ensure that this funding is secured in its area of influence. Apart from lifestyle entrepreneurs, who tend to be highly ethically motivated individuals, having left the industry with which they are most familiar to enter a more fulfilling activity, the private sector spin-ins seem to take two forms. In some cases, the entrepreneur has identified a highly profitable niche in a mainstream market and uses the profitability within that market to cross subsidise low-cost services. In other cases, the private entrepreneur seeks to participate in a mainstream marketplace but in an inclusive and ethically informed manner.

Ethics in the choice of organisational strategy

A social enterprise could operate in any marketplace if it adopts Kim Alter's *service subsidisation model* (Alter, 2007, pp 220-1). This means that the social enterprise can operate in any market, (assuming that it does not conflict with the core objectives of the charity) as long as it creates profit or surplus that can be gifted to the charity. This is the very successful model used by the Salvation Army and its separate trading wing. On the whole, however, charities are more likely to (and should) seek to turn a cost base into an enterprise (the need to cut grass on a charity estate turns into a grass-cutting service to increase the utilisation of the infrastructure); or to utilise existing resources, skills and networks to develop a new business opportunity. This resource-driven entrepreneurship is useful for the charity to ensure that all of its assets are being fully utilised, but also lends knowledge of the marketplace and its players to the charity spin-out that would otherwise limit the new entrant who knows nothing about the business.

Another model suggested by Alter is that of the *market intermediary* (Alter, 2007, p 216). This is most famously exemplified by fair trade organisations, but also covers micro-credit organisations that broker trust as well as finance from the mainstream to the socially and financially excluded. This replicates, and introduces a level of ethics into, mainstream supplier/middleman entrepreneurship.

Alter also suggests an *employment model* (2007, p 218) whereby the beneficiaries of the social enterprise activity are employed by the enterprise. Again, social enterprises like this could operate in any marketplace. A community recycling group, for instance, could, in theory, own and operate a major materials recovery facility and provide employment for disadvantaged staff. Derivatives of this model are the social firm and cooperative structures where the beneficiaries are owners and managers as well as employees. The level of beneficiaries in the organisation varies (with social firms requiring 50% of beneficiaries inside the organisation) but the level of this variation will have a significant impact on the viability of the organisation.

Organisations that are focused on the delivery of public services or those who see the implementation of government policy as their primary role often select the *fee-for-service* model (Alter, 2007, p 219). This model commercialises social services and then sells them to the public sector, or in some cases to individuals who purchase them with their own money or with vouchers from the public sector. This is predominant in sectors such as day care and health and well-being services. Delivering the service well and on behalf of the beneficiaries is the primary social aim of the organisation. In this case, there is rarely a dynamic market (that is, supply/demand) rate for the product or service. The price will be based on the budgets of the government authority rather than the perceived or actual value to the beneficiary. This is the model that is becoming increasingly important as more and more services are commissioned from the third sector.

Once these choices have been made, the organisation still needs to remain innovative. Its model of social change, its choice of marketplace and its organisational strategy will govern much of this activity but its approach to understanding social issues must remain dynamic. Preventing its basic analytical processes from becoming static will help the social enterprise maintain a critical innovative focus. The two key points here are to enrich the way the social issue is perceived and ensure that the problem is not oversimplified or rendered static.

Analysing for innovation: systems skills

Innovation doesn't just happen – it needs investigation and knowledge. This is illustrated in the China case study (Chapter Twelve), where the social entrepreneurs had to develop both a market for yak fur as a material for the clothing industry as well as yak cheese, both products being new for wider national and international audiences.

The way in which a problem or social issue is conceptualised is a critical skill for a social entrepreneur, particularly because the way in which the problem is conceptualised affects the way in which solutions are developed. Developing an open, transparent and inclusive approach to the formulation or construction of a social problem is a core objective. What often happens is that entrepreneurs construct a social problem in their own mind, develop a solution to it, and then seek to implement it. This means that the problem has not necessarily been 'opened up' and considered from a variety of angles – the thinking becomes convergent on a single solution rather than divergent to a number of different possible solutions. (See chapter Four for further information about identifying need.)

Wicked issues

A wicked issue is a social problem in which the various stakeholders can barely agree on what the definition of the problem should be, let alone on what the solution is. Social issues and problems are intrinsically 'wicked' or 'messy', and it is very dangerous for them to be treated as if they were 'tame' and 'benign'. Real world problems have no definitive formulation; no point at which it is definitely solved; solutions are not true or false; there is no test for a solution; every solution contributes to a further social problem; there are no well-defined sets of solutions; wicked problems are unique; they are symptomatic of other problems; they do not have simple causes; they have numerous possible explanations which in turn frame different policy responses; and, in particular, the social enterprise is not allowed to fail in its attempts to solve wicked problems. (Rittel and Webber, 1973). Such wicked issues can be further described with the following six criteria:

Six criteria for wicked problems

1. *You don't understand the problem until you have developed a solution.* Every solution that is offered exposes new aspects of the problem, requiring further adjustments to the potential solutions. There is no definitive statement of 'the problem': these problems are ill-structured and feature an evolving set of interlocking issues and constraints.
2. *There is no stopping rule.* Since there is no definitive 'problem', there is also no definitive 'solution.' The problem-solving process ends when you run out of resources such as time, money or energy, not when an optimal solution emerges.
3. *Solutions are not right or wrong.* They are simply 'better/worse' or 'good enough/ not good enough'. The determination of solution quality is not objective and cannot be derived from following a formula.
4. *Each is essentially unique and novel.* No two wicked problems are alike, and the solutions to them will always be custom designed and fitted. Over time we

can acquire wisdom and experience about the approach to wicked problems, but one is always a beginner in the specifics of a new wicked problem.

5. *Every solution is a 'one-shot operation'.* Every attempt has consequences. This is the 'Catch 22' of wicked problems: you can't learn about the problem without trying solutions, but every solution is expensive and has lasting consequences that may spawn new wicked problems.

6. *There is no given alternative solution.* A host of potential solutions may be devised, but another host are never even thought of. Thus it is a matter of creativity to devise potential solutions, and a matter of judgement to determine which should be pursued and implemented.

There is no quick fix for wicked problems, no glib formula about 'Seven Steps to Crush Social Complexity' or how to 'Tame Your Way to the Top'. The most significant strategy in coping with (rather than solving) and promoting innovative responses is to '*keep the issue wicked*'. It is important that the paradoxes that underlie the social issue are not collapsed into an either/or argument, and that any socially entrepreneurial response, product or service is seen as a prompt for the next question, the next analysis. The four taming strategies (from Conklin, 2005) are often misused as ways of dealing with the problem of wicked issues, but Conklin is clear in his work that these strategies are the wrong strategies and that they should be avoided.

Four taming strategies to be avoided

1. *Lock down the problem definition.* Develop a description of a related problem that you can solve, and declare that to be the problem. Specify objective parameters by which to measure the solution's success.

2. *Cast the problem as 'just like' a previous problem that has been solved.* Ignore or filter out evidence that complicates the picture.

3. *Give up on trying to find a good solution.* Just follow orders, do your job and try not to get in trouble.

4. *Declare that there are just a few possible solutions, and focus on selecting from among them.* A specific way to do this is to frame the problem in 'either/or' terms.

While it may seem appealing in the short run, attempting to tame a wicked problem will always fail in the long run. The problem will simply reassert itself, perhaps in a different guise, as if nothing had been done; or worse, the tame solution will exacerbate the problem.

Enriching the issue

One process that can be picked up on by the social entrepreneur and can be used to both analyse a situation with numerous stakeholders and ensure that an issue is 'kept wicked' is employing rich pictures. Rich pictures were developed as part of Peter Checkland's soft systems methodology for gathering information about a complex situation (Checkland, 1981). Rich pictures are a graphical means of representing a situation, which draws on the whole individual in a group situation to represent as creatively as possible the various factors, actors and relationships that act on a particular social situation.

The process of developing a rich picture is more important than the rich picture itself; it is a group process rather than an individual one. Each member of the group seeks to represent their view of the situation in question in a graphical manner and several iterations of the picture-drawing process will help. These pictures are then compared with those produced by other members of the group (and even people who are not members of the group could be encouraged to represent what they see of the same situation). The comparison process is based around discussing what is similar in the pictures and exploring why the pictures differ, in order to understand each other's world view and develop a sense of the commonality of the world views, without necessarily choosing one picture as the 'definitive' representation – there is no definitive representation. Dependencies on other situations that are related can be explored, and the boundaries of the issue can be (tentatively) established and scenarios can be built that address the multiple facets of the issue – keeping it wicked and avoiding taming it.

The Open University provides a fine publicly available online course on rich pictures within the systems analysis field (Anon, 2009b). The course material has the following recommendations about significant traps in thinking and analysis. An awareness of these traps in thinking across a whole organisation will help to avoid the taming of wicked issues.

Traps that limit innovative thinking

- *Trap 1 – representing the problem and not the situation.* This trap is one of the most fundamental mistakes that can be made in this process. The whole point of a rich picture is to represent all that is possible to depict about the situation, especially drawing on the insight and resources of other people. To identify the problem within the picture, or to include only the elements that seem problematic, is to prune out potentially important elements of the complexity.
- *Trap 2 – the impoverished rich picture.* A distinguishing feature of rich pictures that turn out to be useful seems to be that they are just what they say they are – rich. If I take usefulness as the criterion, the useful rich pictures are the ones bursting with interest and activity.
- *Trap 3 – interpretation, structure, and analysis.* If an interpretation or analysis is deliberately imposed on a situation (and the rich picture that represents it), then the possibility of seeing other potentially more interesting features later is precluded. Remember the rich picture is a representation of the complexity. If that complexity is structured, it is no longer being represented as experienced.
- *Trap 4 – words and wordiness.* Our education system encourages the use of lots of words, but these can also hide meaning. The use of lots of words makes

the rich picture less rich. Part of the later use of a rich picture might include looking for patterns, and words reduce the opportunity do so later.

- *Trap 5 – the final version trap.* Rich pictures are never finished. New realisations and insights will crop up. As the organisation or group come to appreciate more and more of the complexity within a situation, the rich picture(s) should be updated and revised, and the activities, services or products that have been developed on the basis of these rich pictures should also be accordingly revised.

Implementing innovation: mind-set shifts

Getting innovation to happen

Much is written, and said, about the importance of developing an entrepreneurial culture. This is easier said than done, and more is said than done. The important part of developing an entrepreneurial culture is to ensure that the talk turns into practice. This means that the culture needs to have artefacts as evidence of the culture becoming embedded. Cultural artefacts are the evidence of culture being transmitted, making the transience of organisation 'talk' into something more substantial. If an organisation professes to promote a culture of innovation and entrepreneurship, the manager should look for artefacts that support the presence of these assertions. Such artefacts of innovation could include a flat organisational structure, employees who are active in strategic direction, teamwork that is active between units or disciplines within the organisation, different services that come together to focus on the client in a holistic manner and close communication between staff of all ranks – the chief executive is not too important to speak directly with cleaners, no matter how large the organisation. The professed culture of the organisation is found in its artefacts, yet, conversely, the organisation itself is an artefact of the mind. The social enterprise, therefore, is enacted each day by its staff, clients and stakeholders, so just implementing systems and rules do not guarantee an innovative culture.

Culbert (1996) picks up the concept of 'artefact' in treating the organisation as an artefact of the mind. Culbert seeks, in his book, to define the skills of managing as 'staging the conditions for others to be effective' (p 160). This seems to be very close to the required skills set of a social entrepreneur, and the book has been very formative in this author's own experience of social entrepreneurship and teaching the subject. Indeed, Culbert provides a profoundly social concept of management when he exhorts the reader to 'stop trying to get people to be what you want them to be. Engage them where they actually are' (p 33). To this end, the next section comprises an extended summary of Culbert's work, drawing out in particular the skills that Culbert describes and how they relate to innovation in social enterprises.

How to achieve change when the change agent has no significant power

While Culbert's concern is the change in corporate organisations, the same concerns that he deals with can be extended to change agents within social entrepreneurship, where the social entrepreneur is seeking to effect systemic change, often from positions of limited power and resources (entrepreneurs classically rearrange other people's resources rather than their own), in some mysterious way described but only scarcely explained in Gladwell's 'tipping point' (Gladwell, 2001). In addition, the social entrepreneur doesn't just seek change within the comfortable boundaries of the corporation; instead the social entrepreneur seeks to influence other organisations, institutions and systems, even societies, way outside their personal control.

Culbert begins with pointing out that the new management techniques that are popular in business schools, and those now being imposed on public services and social enterprises, are based on a similar set of principles:

- total organisation teamwork;
- thoughtfulness and flexibility at the customer contact point;
- sensitivity and quick reaction to marketplace changes;
- the importance of everyone understanding the big picture;
- leadership from within the ranks;
- attentiveness to the human element;
- constructive politics and trusting relationship with a dedicated and informed workforce;
- globalised thinking and strategic input in the execution and implementation of company action.

So is 30 years of management science summarised, and should all these factors be in place, then social enterprises (as well as mainstream businesses) will be wonderful, humane and inventive places.

Culbert goes on to stress the importance of developing an 'outsider's perspective'. This is closely related to Pinchot's intrapreneurship work (Pinchot, 1985) and this author's own work on extrapreneurship in supporting and developing social enterprises in the context of public sector organisations (Curtis and Minto, 2008). An intrapreneur is seen as an employee in a typical hierarchical and structured organisation who exhibits entrepreneurial behaviours contributing to business success and innovation.

Opening up opportunities for the exhibition of entrepreneurial behaviour within a controlled, policy-driven, role- and procedure-based organisation is important if innovative environments are to be generated wherein 'entrepreneurial' activity and competences can develop and flourish. Pinchot published a bill of rights for intrapreneurs in 1999 (Pinchot and Pellman, 1999). He suggests that all employees should be allocated 10% of their time to pursue new ideas they believe may be useful to a social outcome. They should be allowed to form a new enterprising activity if their salary can be covered by revenue from the new customers. The intrapreneurial team that has created a solvent social enterprise has a quasi-ownership right to continue operating it – it cannot be taken and given to others without cause and due process. Every employee should have the right to join an intraprise, provided the intraprise is agreeable and is able and willing to pay him or her salary. The intrapreneurs should also have the right to deposit revenue and assets in the home organisation, where it cannot be appropriated by any other entity except as the result of due process or corporate taxation at normal rates. The intrapreneurs should also have the right to control spend or dispose of the capital and revenue of their activity as they see fit for the furtherance of their work.

These rules set ground conditions by which the potential innovator can be seen to share in the (social and financial) proceeds of the innovation. Along with this, the social innovator may also wish to consider Pinchot's guidance for effective intrapreneurship, his Ten Commandments:

- Build your team, intrapreneuring is not a solo activity.
- Share credit widely.
- Ask for advice before you ask for resources.
- Underpromise and overdeliver – publicity triggers the corporate immune system.
- Do any job needed to make your dream work, regardless of your job description.
- Remember it is easier to ask for forgiveness than for permission.
- Keep the best interests of the company and its customers in mind, especially when you have to bend the rules or circumvent the bureaucracy.
- Come to work each day willing to be fired.
- Be true to your goals, but be realistic about how to achieve them.
- Honour and educate your sponsors.

Conclusion

This chapter has considered how a social enterprise can be innovative without harming the principles of equity, openness and accountability that underpin ethical public service. It has been established that the way a problem is conceptualised fundamentally affects the type, and scope, of innovation that takes place. This means that ethical innovative practice must start with the ethics of framing the social problem. This requires attention to how complex social issues are constructed. The perception of the problem and how it is constructed should be enriched through collaborative diagramming techniques such as rich pictures to prevent the issue from being 'tamed' or oversimplified. Taming a problem results in a small part of the issue being addressed and, ultimately, the real situation is inadequately addressed.

Framing the social issue in a collaborative, and enriching, manner should lead to an honest and dynamic response to the social issue, which will then inform the choice of the model of social change employed. Carefully considering the model of social change will then influence the marketplace and organisational strategy of the social enterprise. In all the case studies in this volume the social entrepreneurs have addressed the issues in collaborative ways, responding to issues and needs in creative and innovative ways.

References

Aiken, M. (2007) *What is the role of social enterprise in finding, creating and maintaining employment for disadvantaged groups?*, London: Office of the Third Sector.

Albury, D. (2005) 'Fostering innovation in public services', *Public Money and Management*, vol 25, pp 51-6.

Alter, S. K. (2007) 'New models: social enterprise models and their mission and money relationships', in A. Nicholls (ed) *Social entrepreneurship: New models of sustainable social change*, Oxford: Oxford University Press, pp 205-32.

Anon (2009a) *Greyston Bakery guiding principles* (www.greystonbakery.com/pdf/greyston-bakery-guiding-principles.pdf).

Anon (2009b) *Managing complexity: A systems approach – introduction* (http://openlearn.open.ac.uk/course/view.php?id=3336&topic=all).

Baumol, W. J. (2002) *The free-market innovation machine*, Princeton, NJ: Princeton University Press.

Bryan, S., Neck, C. and Goldsby, M. (1998) 'The scoop on Ben & Jerry's Inc.: an examination of corporate social responsibility', *Journal of Managerial Psychology*, vol 5/6, no 13, pp 387-93.

Checkland, P. (1981) *Systems thinking, systems practice*, Chichester: John Wiley & Sons.

Conklin, J. (2005) *Building shared understanding of wicked problems*, Chichester: Wiley.

Culbert, S. (1996) *Mind-set management: The heart of leadership*, Oxford: Oxford University Press.

Curtis, T. (2004) *Best value review for landfill tax funding arrangements*, Aberdeen: Aberdeen Forward and Aberdeen Countryside Project, Enviros Consulting Limited.

Curtis, T. and Minto, I. (2008) *Cultural shift: South east academic research outcomes*, Guildford: South East of England Development Agency.

De Bono, E. (1968) *New think: The use of lateral thinking in the generation of new ideas*, New York: Basic Books.

Fagerberg, J. (2004) 'Innovation: a guide to the literature', in J. Fagerberg, D. Mowery and R. Nelson (eds) *The Oxford handbook of innovations*, Oxford: Oxford University Press, pp 1-26.

Freeman, C. (1997) *The economics of industrial innovation*, Cambridge, MA: MIT Press.

Fuglsang, L. and Mattsson, J. (2009) 'An integrative model of care ethics in public innovation', *The Service Industries Journal*, vol 29, no 1, pp 21-34.

Gladwell, M. (2001) *The tipping point: How little things can make a big difference*, London: Abacus.

Glor, E. (2003) 'Innovation traps: risks and challenges in thinking about innovation', *The Innovation Journal: A special issue on the ethics of innovation*, vol 8, no 3.

Hanekamp, G. (2007) *Business ethics of innovation*, Berlin and Heidelberg: Springer Verlag.

Hartley, J. (2005) 'Innovation in governance and public services: past and present, *Public Money and Management*, vol 25, no 1, pp 27-34.

Henry, J. (2001) *Creativity and perception in management*, London: Sage.

Leadbeater, C. (2007) *Social enterprise and social innovation: Strategies for the next ten years*, London: Cabinet Office.

Leiter, J. (2005) 'Structural isomorphism in Australian nonprofit organizations', *Voluntas: International Journal of Voluntary and Nonprofit Organizations*, vol 16, no 1, p 31.

Lowe, R. and Marriott, S. (2007) *Enterprise: Entrepreneurship and innovation*, Oxford: Butterworth-Heinemann.

Luecke, R. and Katz, R. (2003) *Managing creativity and innovation*, Boston, MA: Harvard Business School Press.

Moore, M. (1995) *Creating public value: Strategic management in government*, Cambridge, MA: Harvard University Press.

Moore, M., Sparrow, M. and Spelman, W. (1997) 'Innovation in policing: from production line to jobs shops', in A. Altchuler and R. Behn (eds), *Innovation in American government*, Washington, DC: Brookings Institution.

Mulgan, G. and Albury, D. (2003) *Innovation in the public sector*, London: Cabinet Office.

Mulgan, G., Rushanara, A., Halkett. R, and Sanders, B. (2007) *In and out of sync: The challenge of growing social innovations*, London: National Endowment for Science, Technology and the Arts (NESTA).

Newman, J., Raine, J. and Skelcher, C. (2001) 'Transforming local government: innovation and modernization', *Public Money and Management*, vol 21, no 2, pp 61-8.

Nicholls, A. (2007) *What is the future of social enterprise in ethical markets?*, London: Cabinet Office.

Nicholls, J. (2007) *Why measuring and communicating social value can help social enterprise become more competitive*, London: Cabinet Office.

Parker, S. (2009) *More than good ideas: The power of innovation in local government*, London: Improvement and Development Agency and NESTA (www. youngfoundation.org/files/images/publications/More_than_good_ideas.pdf).

Pinchot, G. (1985) *Intrapreneuring: Why you don't have to leave the corporation to become an entrepreneur*, New York: Harper and Row.

Pinchot, G. and Pellman, R. (1999) *Intrapreneuring in action*, San Francisco, CA: Berrett-Koehler.

Rittel, H. and Webber, M. (1973) 'Dilemmas in a general theory of planning', *Policy Sciences*, vol 4, pp 155-69 (www.uctc.net/mwebber/Rittel+Webber+Dilemmas+General_ Theory_of_Planning.pdf). [Reprinted (1984) N. Cross (ed) *Developments in design methodology*, Chichester: John Wiley & Sons, pp 135-44.]

Schine, G. (2003) *How to succeed as a lifestyle entrepreneur*, Chicago: Kaplan Business Dearborn Trade Publishing.

Sellers, M. (2003) 'Privatisation morphs into "publicization": businesses look at lot like government', *Public Administration*, vol 81, no 3, pp 607-20.

Stinchcombe, A. (1965) 'Social structure and organizations', in J. March (ed) *Handbook of organizations*, Chicago: Rand-McNally, pp 142-93.

Taylor, W. and Labarre, P. (2006) *Mavericks at work: Why the most original minds in business win*, New York: HarperCollins.

Tidd, J., Bessant, J. and Pavitt, K. (2005) *Managing innovation: Integrating technological market and organisational change*, Chichester: John Wiley & Sons.

Trott, P. (2002) *Innovation management and new product development*, Harlow, Essex: Pearson Education.

Vries, K. (1977) 'The entrepreneurial personality: a person at the crossroads', *Journal of Management Studies*, vol 14, no 1, pp 34-57.

Westall, A. (2007) *How can innovation in social enterprise be understood, encouraged and enabled?*, London: Cabinet Office.

Woodward, J. (1965) *Industrial organisation: Theory and practice*, Oxford: Oxford University Press.

NINE

Leadership and management skills development in social enterprises

Jon Griffith

Introduction

This chapter looks at the leadership and management skills required to run organisations, or parts of organisations, and how these skills are developed. Are these skills sufficient for running social enterprises and if not, what special skills are needed, and how do people develop them?

We first have to consider the variations between organisational types: for example, armies are obviously different from shops, and this affects how they are run. However, there have been debates throughout history about the extent to which there are general principles or practices of running an organisation, and to what extent leadership and management skills vary according to organisation type.

There is a second area of debate about the differences between leadership and management: do some organisations or activities require more leadership than management and others more management than leadership? How does this variation apply to social enterprises?

Finally, there is the difference between social enterprises, collectively, as one type of organisation, and other types of organisation we can identify: what distinctions can be drawn between their special leadership and management needs, and those of organisations in general?

The chapter begins with a brief historical review of leadership and management before examining the major issues in the subject, then moves on to consider how issues change as organisations grow, and ends with a discussion of how social entrepreneurs and managers develop their skills.

Leadership and management skills: a historical view

Ideas about leadership and management have changed continually over time and across cultures. The following advice is attributed to Lao Tsu, the originator of Taoism (born c 600 BC):

> To lead people, walk beside them ....As for the best leaders, the people do not notice their existence. The next best, the people honor and praise. The next, the people fear; and the next, the people hate.... When the best leader's work is done the people say, 'We did it ourselves!'

Many centuries later, Machiavelli (1469-1527) wrote:

> A prince should therefore have no other aim or thought, nor take up any other thing for his study but war and its organization and discipline, for that is the only art that is necessary to one who commands. (www.quotationspage.com/quote/24517.html)

In the past hundred years or so, many researchers, writers, philosophers, teachers, consultants, and some leaders and managers themselves, have tried more systematically to describe what organisation leaders and managers do, how they do it, and how they learn to do it, often with the intention of spreading ideas about good practice or sound principles.

For example, Frederick Taylor (1856-1915), wrote in his introduction to *The principles of scientific management*:

> This paper has been written ... to prove that the best management is a true science, resting upon clearly defined laws, rules, and principles, as a foundation. And further to show that the fundamental principles of scientific management are applicable to all kinds of human activities, from our simplest individual acts to the work of our great corporations, which call for the most elaborate cooperation. (Taylor, 1911, p 7)

In the same period, Henri Fayol (1841-1925) identified the five elements of management as:

- planning
- organising
- commanding
- co-ordinating, and
- controlling (Fayol, 1917).

He also produced a list of 14 principles of management, about matters like authority, equity, and esprit de corps, which continue to be a cause of debate: some people approve of the structure his principles provide, while others disparage them as dictatorial, or patronising.

Other influential 20th century writers, such as Mayo (1933), McGregor (1960), Herzberg (1966), Maslow (1970), Ouchi (1982), Deming (1986) and Lewin (1997), addressed, from a range of perspectives, the importance of treating people well at work, in order to get the best out of them, and helped produce a dominant, humanistic view of management. However, opposing views did not disappear: management by objectives, action-centred leadership, and business process re-engineering are examples of ideas which take a harder line on management or leadership tasks, and do not place people at the centre; and there has been a continuing strand of thinking which asserts 'management's right to manage', articulated most forcibly by the employer's side in the British miners' strike in the 1980s.

In 1982, Tom Peters and Robert Waterman published *In search of excellence*, where they converted the seven elements of organisational effectiveness espoused by their employer, the McKinsey management consultancy (namely, structure, strategy, systems, style of management, skills – corporate strengths, staff, and shared values) into eight themes of 'excellent' organisations:

1. a bias for action, active decision making – 'getting on with it';
2. close to the customer – learning from the people served by the business;
3. autonomy and entrepreneurship – fostering innovation and nurturing 'champions';
4. productivity through people – treating rank-and-file employees as a source of quality;
5. hands-on, value-driven – management philosophy that guides everyday practice – management showing its commitment;
6. stick to the knitting – stay with the business that you know;
7. simple form, lean staff – some of the best companies have minimal HQ staff;
8. Simultaneous loose-tight properties – autonomy in shop-floor activities plus centralised values (as summarised by Chapman, 2009).

They offered not only a new view of management and leadership tasks, but a new way of discussing them, unconstrained by any effort to be either scientific, in an orthodox sense, or humanistic: they were just sharing their impressions of what worked. *In search of excellence* prefigured the idea of 'the learning organisation' and another book, *The fifth discipline* (Senge, 1990), which retains similar influence today on thinking about management and leadership.

Much writing about leadership and management emphasises universals, that is, general behaviours that managers or leaders are observed to adopt, with good or bad effects, and skills which can be used in any setting. Yet even within this literature it's often acknowledged that one important, universal way of managing or leading effectively is to be attentive to the unique characteristics of the organisation's own situation. This has important implications for social entrepreneurs and managers in social enterprises.

Leadership and management in different types of organisations

We can assume that social enterprises have some things in common with other types of organisations. In some respects with conventional commercial organisations (especially small businesses and family firms), in other respects with community or voluntary organisations, and perhaps even with some public sector organisations, we can assume at least some common ground in how they are led and managed across these sectoral boundaries, and therefore in the skills needed to lead and manage them.

For example, all organisations need to:

- know what their main work is;
- communicate this, internally and externally;
- assemble resources to carry out their work, including money and people;
- maintain their resources;
- monitor and evaluate their work;
- find out what is happening in their environment;
- plan future work, including changes.

Of course, the organisation and its work are led and managed differently, according to type and setting, so a church will be led and managed differently from a government department or a bank or a charity shop. But equally, parish churches are led and managed differently from each other, as are government departments and banks and charity shops. On the other hand, it's true that organisations which do similar things end up seeming to be similar to each other, at least to outsiders. So all high street banks seem to operate in much the same way, and to be led and managed in much the same way, and this style of operation can be easily distinguished from the way churches or charity shops operate. (This phenomenon has been described as 'institutional isomorphism', from the Greek *iso* , meaning 'the same', and *morphos*, which means 'shape'; see Di Maggio and Powell, 1983).

Nevertheless, the variations between organisations of the same type are important, because they provide the opportunity for different approaches to leadership and management, and for debate about the positives and negatives of different approaches. So some churches are independent, and some are a part of larger hierarchies; in the latter case, local church leaders may be more or less willing to conform to establishment views. Some charity shops are controlled entirely at the local level with the manager deciding how to organise things, for instance, who to hire or when to open. Another charity shop in the same street might be entirely controlled by a head office located elsewhere.

Distinctive leadership and management tasks in social enterprises

There are a number of different ideas about social enterprises which might affect their leadership and management, for example:

- they ought to achieve a social goal through trading in a market place;
- they ought not to be dependent on grants or subsidies;
- they ought to be autonomous;
- they ought to behave in a particularly responsible way towards their employees and other stakeholders;
- they ought to involve employees and other stakeholders in the governance of the organisation;
- the governance of the organisation ought to be democratic;
- they ought to be owned by the community.

Even more important than these views, however, are the practices of individual social enterprises themselves. We can see from the evidence presented elsewhere in this book that social enterprises vary greatly in many ways, in size, in age, in origin, in purpose, in complexity, in culture, in ownership, and so on. This means that they are almost bound to do things in different ways, and in different styles, so we can expect to see wide variations between them in how they are led and managed. But they have something important in common with each other. A defining characteristic of social enterprises is their claim to be different from other kinds of enterprise. They don't make money for the sake of it, they make money in order to do good, and sometimes in the process of doing good. They don't just do good either; they do good in a way that can be sustained, ultimately, without relying on third parties for handouts. This is the 'double bottom-line': social enterprises are not like conventional commercial companies, because the enterprise is not satisfied with turning a profit, or paying the proprietor a living wage and breaking even; it is committed to the achievement of a social purpose as well. Unless *both* bottom lines are seen to return a 'profit' at the end of the accounting year, the enterprise has failed.

One implication of this status is that the overall leadership and management task involves an element of balancing objectives which are by definition in tension with each other, and requires something other than ordinary leadership and management skill. Another way of saying this is that social enterprises are 'hybrid' organisations, agencies that straddle sectors or types, so they involve an added layer of complexity in decision making, planning, and so on. If this is true, then standard methods of leadership and management skill development may not be good enough for social enterprises.

Leadership or management, or both?

Fashions change. Once upon a time, the elites of the Anglo-Saxon world were interested only in leadership, and management was something to be left to minions. During the 20th century, a 'science' of management emerged, mainly in response to industrialisation, and held the attention of thinkers and doers for several decades. For a few decades after the Second World War, ideas like 'management by objectives' and 'management by walking about' vied with 'action centred leadership' and 'servant leadership' for precedence.

Over the past 20 years, leadership has been in vogue again, as the more important missing ingredient in organisations and institutions, perhaps as a result of distaste for supposed 'managerialism', with its connotation of inflexible, bureaucratic, over-rational control. For example, since publishing *The seven habits of highly effective people* in 1990, Stephen R. Covey has developed a philosophy of leadership, as distinct from management, in a series of books which have sold many millions of copies. Similarly, John Kotter, in *What leaders really do*, has argued for more clarity in the distinction between management in leadership, and sees organisations and institutions as both over managed and under led.

> Leadership is different from management, but not for the reasons most people think. It has nothing to do with having charisma or other exotic personality traits. It is not the province of the chosen few. Nor is leadership necessarily better than management or a replacement for it. Both are necessary for success in a complex and volatile business environment. (Kotter, 1999, p 51)

A consensus may now be forming, across industries and sectors, and between theorists and practitioners, that leadership and management are different but sometimes overlapping sets of practices, behaviours and skills, that both of them are bound to be present in organisations and institutions, and that both of them can be learned. However, we should not be surprised by further declarations in favour of one and against the other, as this sells books.

Stages of growth in organisations

Organisations change over time. Commercial empires began as market stalls, large government departments may have originally been a single desk in another ministry and a charity with thousands of volunteers was once a conversation around a kitchen table. We can produce and critique formal theories about the life-stages of organisations but even without these, change is evident: prices go up and down, and so do personnel and properties.

When a commercial enterprise is new, it may have a handful of people earning an income from it, rather than a sole trader, but it's not unusual for one person or two people to have a dominant interest (cooperatives are the exception to this rule).

How the enterprise is run will depend greatly on the one or two people with the biggest stake and not necessarily on their training in leadership and management (they may not have any, nor any relevant previous experience), nor even on their ideas about leadership and management, though they may have some of these. They are more likely to want to get the work done well enough to stay afloat and grow, by any means necessary. This may involve sacrifices, and asking others to share in these sacrifices. The principals may learn constantly from what they are doing, or read management books on the beach, or get themselves a mentor, or find some suitable training courses, but none of this is guaranteed to happen.

At a later stage of development, the situation will be different. Paid employees of an established enterprise will have rights to, or at least expectations of, for example, training and development; and they won't be willing to make the same kind of sacrifices as members of a founding team.

This is not the same across sectors. If a local authority sets up a new unit, even if it is run by a single employee, this member of staff will expect the same terms and conditions as their colleagues in other departments. They will expect management and leadership from others, and a clear expression of the management and leadership tasks they themselves are required to carry out; it's not likely to be a process of discovery and response to market demand.

This suggests a spectrum of formality in the leadership and management of organisations, and some variation between organisations as they grow, according to sector. Voluntary organisations may be placed at many points along this spectrum, but in their earliest stages we can expect a difference from commercial enterprises. There is more often likely to be a larger group of people involved in the formation of a voluntary organisation, because the one or two initiators will see it as advantageous to involve other people, rather than keep them out.

Social enterprises straddle sector boundaries here too; those with a strong urge to establish themselves in a market niche may see a good reason for minimising the number of people they involve at the outset, unlike the initiators of many conventional voluntary or community organisations, especially if they see an income-earning role for themselves in the enterprise. At later stages in their development, the distinctiveness of social enterprise leadership and management may become more or less pronounced.

In some cases, well-established social enterprises may have come up with sophisticated ways of ensuring they achieve their double bottom line objectives and so stand out from private and voluntary sector counterparts in the same industry, for example by combining performance-related rewards for staff with a higher than average level of user-involvement. The management systems may be different, but they will have emerged from the understanding by key people of the need for different management systems, and their ability to invent and maintain them.

In other cases, a social enterprise may be indistinguishable from public or voluntary sector organisations in the same field. The double bottom line may exist on paper and even in practice, but the real differences between organisations may be so minimal, for example between residential care providers in the same local authority area, that the management and leadership practices are identical.

When organisations get very big (for their field or sector), another set of factors begins to affect leadership and management. They begin to compete much more intensely with other employers for leaders and senior managers who have the kind of previous experience they are looking for. In the past 20 years in the UK, this has meant a growing third sector, including social enterprises, recruiting increasingly from the commercial and public sector, as the early leaders and senior managers of successful organisations move on.

How are leadership and management skills developed?

Generically, we can assume that part of the answer to this question can be found in the ever-increasing number of business schools across the globe, the growth in training courses, and the proliferation of books about leadership and management; they would not exist if they were not meeting a demand, and part of the demand is likely to be for skills development.

However, there are some opposing views. The more radical and perhaps old-fashioned view is that some elements of leadership and management can't be taught; that people are born with aptitudes for leadership and management; or that these skills develop very early in life, which will equip them to be successful leaders or managers in the future. A less radical view is that people may be able to develop, well into adulthood, the skills needed to lead and manage organisations, but that they will best do this through activities that are not directly pointed towards that goal. So, for instance, learning to climb mountains or do equations is a better preparation for leading and managing than going on a leadership or management course. However, the most common opposing view is that, like many other skills, leading and managing can only be learned by doing it.

Active skill development in leadership and management takes some distinct forms:

- courses for people with no relevant experience; these involve the transmission of knowledge, some simulation, possibly placements in real work settings, reflection on experience, and the articulation of an improved understanding of leadership and management roles;
- professional development for people with relevant experience, involving mainly similar learning processes, but with a focus on their experience and how it can be integrated;
- explicit learning processes which are not courses, such as supervision, mentoring, professional consultation, action learning, peer groups, and so on;
- learning processes which are not so explicit, such as getting help informally from other people, learning by doing, experimenting with new behaviours, etc.

It has never been clear what works best. This is partly because it is hard to measure improvement in leadership and management skills, and partly because different ways of learning work more or less well for different people and at different stages of people's professional lives.

Some aspects of performance may be quantifiable, but others are not, so although organisations typically devote much energy and effort to gathering information about skill development, this information is not reliable, and organisations either carry on with what they already do, or change continually. What compounds this problem is that even where it is clear that leadership or management skills have been improved, we cannot know for sure how this has come about. Of course, those responsible for skill development, human resources departments, internal change agents, and especially consultants, claim (and may genuinely believe) that their own work has been significant, but this is often impossible to establish.

So what can be safely and reasonably concluded about active skill development in management and leadership? First, that claims are suspect unless it can be shown *how* a learning process has helped someone lead or manage better. This will usually mean that someone concerned can say *what* has changed, and the relationship between the change and the learning process can be traced, even if only tentatively. Second, that normal expectation about evidence may nevertheless need to be put aside. What people say about their own learning may need to be taken on trust, and the testing of their skill development taken slowly, gently, and not confrontationally.

These conclusions are, of course, mutually contradictory. They encapsulate a tension at the heart of skills development generally, between the often different interests of the individual and the group, and this tension is at its sharpest in the domain of leadership and management skills. When individuals are committed to improving these skills, their commitment is both to the organisation and their own benefit, and it is doubly hard for people to honestly evaluate their own contribution to improving an organisation they care about.

Social enterprises: a special case?

Leaders and managers do what they must in the public sector, and what they can in the marketplace. The 'third sector', however, has for many years presented a challenge, to theorists and practitioners alike. How should its leaders and managers behave, when their behaviour is not dictated by the law, nor determined by the market?

For roughly the first half of the 20th century in England, people responsible for charity, the collection of resources and their application to charitable objects, were governed in their actions by ideas about trusteeship, stewardship, and administration. Some of this was a matter of law, but it was also a matter of culture. Oxfam opened its first charity shop in 1942, and the third sector was firmly on the road to the change embodied in today's social enterprises. Since this time, there has been an ever-growing global industry in organisation, management, and leadership development, and a continuing debate about how far the needs of the third sector can be met by this generic provision.

Across the organisational world, leadership and management tasks and roles vary immensely, from running the boards of multinational corporations, to keeping one-person businesses going. A wide range of leadership and management skills is needed to perform these tasks and roles, so skills development at one end of the spectrum might mean a multimillion pound programme for hundreds of people over several years and at the other end of the spectrum, a sole proprietor attending a free half-day workshop. We can identify some of this range of need through observing the range of provision, but we can be confident that some needs remain unmet. There are usually skills gaps in any economy, and it is often claimed of specific industries (such as manufacturing in the UK in the 1980s) that there are serious weaknesses in leadership and management skills.

To the extent that social enterprises are part of the larger economy, and require some of the same leadership and management skills as other organisations, some of these skills will be developed in the same way as they are in enterprises in general. So, for example, there is a generic need for people in senior positions to understand both the market they are in, and their own organisation's internal world, to be able to engage with others inside and outside the organisation in planning, mobilising resources, and producing goods or services, to communicate in different directions, and to maintain stability and confidence (although this is just one way of describing a set of leadership and management skills; there have been many different attempts to summarise these skills since people began analysing leadership and management).

Similarly, people have developed these skills through a wide range of processes. Early life experience, general education, vocational training, apprenticeship, practice, feedback, trial and error, going on courses, tailored individual programmes, mentoring, supervision, unstructured learning, reading, retreats, reflection (both on and in action), contemplation, meditation, conversations with others, and, occasionally, the straightforward application of thinking to a real-world problem. It would be surprising if, on the whole, these skills were developed by people in social enterprises differently from the way they are developed by people generally. It is possible, however, that as a group, the kind of people attracted to working in social enterprises have some learning preferences that are different from the norm.

There is, however, one further distinction between organisations as whole and third sector organisations as a subset. Third sector organisations are usually much smaller than their industry average. If we take an industry as a whole, most social enterprises within it will be at the small-medium end of the range. There are some exceptions: wine cooperatives in the South of France and Northern Italy are bigger on average than their privately owned counterparts, and many housing associations in the UK are now larger than local government landlords. However, in most parts of the economy, social enterprises are still relatively small. This means that, in general, people in social enterprises do not need to develop the special skills required to lead or manage large organisations.

At the same time, social enterprises carry out the same range of work as enterprises in general (or almost the same range) and this means there is a 'long thin' population of social enterprise leaders and managers, across many different industries, without enough 'critical mass' to constitute a viable market for specialist leadership and management skill development in such industries as retailing, catering or hospitality. Their choices will be limited to developing their skills alongside the leaders and managers of ordinary commercial enterprises, or alongside leaders and managers of other social enterprises in other industries.

Developing skills for leading and managing social enterprises

The argument so far, then, suggests that there is nothing special about the leadership and management skills required to run social enterprises. Their leaders and managers need the same skills as their counterparts in other (small and medium-sized) enterprises, and they can (and do) develop these skills in the same way as everyone else.

Against this argument, we are faced both with the double bottom line, claimed to be a distinctive feature of social enterprise, although we may want to question this and the relatively small size of most social enterprises, which means they don't have the capital to create conventional bureaucracies.

One attempted solution to these twin problems has been the production of technical aids, like measures of social return on investment, to build systems capable of handling greater complexity, rather than relying on individuals to develop exceptional skills. The problem created, in turn, is that more complex systems themselves require the development of new human skills to make best use of them. The danger here is that the recognition of complexity leads to the development of enhanced technical, or even technocratic skills, rather than an improvement in people's ability to make sound judgements about priorities, risks and action.

It is in this context that, since the mid 1990s, many courses have been started by universities and training providers in the UK, the US, and elsewhere, in an effort to fill an apparent gap in leadership and management skills among social enterprises. These courses have typically combined conceptual elements with mainly generic tools for use in leading or managing enterprises, and opportunities to practise (with feedback) activities like business planning. The social enterprise sector has itself helped create some of these courses, but others have been created by universities and training providers alone to meet what they see as a demand in the market place. We should not forget that universities and training providers are themselves enterprises, and some of them see themselves as social enterprises, and essentially no different from the organisations whose members attend their courses.

Conclusion

The 'double bottom line' is the strongest concept so far articulated to explain what social enterprises do, and how they operate, and there is a large overlap between this idea and the idea of 'hybridity', with its implications of difficulty or complexity. If this is the most important feature of social enterprise, it seems likely that management, rather than leadership, is the area of most distinctive challenge for social enterprises in developing skills.

Recently a group of educators in this field has suggested that specialist non-profit management education has now had its day, because of changes in and around the organisations, in the people who hold responsible positions within them, and in the routes available for learning and development (Mordaunt et al, 2007).

These changes have included the growth of quality standards, new regulations, increasing demands for transparency, accountability and user involvement, more formal collaboration between organisations, professionalisation of roles, the arrival of people from the public and private sectors as managers and board members and a wider acceptance of some management ideas and language – previously seen as alien.

This chapter suggests abandoning the search for traits, charisma and transformation in favour of people making things happen, being influential, leading without authority, self-managing, and having an underlying psychological capability in reflecting on and changing roles and relationships rather than being subject to them. It also suggests that education has to move beyond the purely cognitive for this to happen.

These seem like promising behaviours for managing in any situation, not just social enterprises. They suggest a return to a kind of learning that has the person at its centre, rather than a radically new educational departure. But is this a realistic approach, compatible with consistently producing the right results in relation to both bottom lines? Perhaps, as ever, this approach will work for those organisations, whether big or small, which devote time and money to developing people's skills. For organisations whose resources are stretched, this will be a challenge. Can learning opportunities be brought to the workplace, in an accessible form, for groups, and not just individuals? The designers and providers of management and leadership skills development programmes are not conspicuously ready for this change, and social enterprises may have to organise their own learning for some time to come.

References

Chapman, A. (2009) *Tom Peters – in search of excellence* (www.businessballs.com/tompetersinsearchofexcellence.htm).

Covey, S. (1990) *The seven habits of highly effective people*, New York, NY: Fireside.

Deming, W. (1986) *Out of the crisis*, Cambridge, MA: MIT Press.

Di Maggio, P. and Powell, W. (1983) 'The iron cage revisited: institutional isomorphism and collective rationality in organizational fields', *American Sociological Review*, vol 48, pp 147-60.

Fayol, H. (1917) *Administration industrielle et générale: prévoyance, organisation, commandement, coordination, controle*, Paris: H. Dunod and E. Pinat.

Herzberg, F. (1966) *Work and the nature of man*, Cleveland, OH: Holland.

Kotter, J. (1999) *What leaders really do*, Boston, MA: Harvard Business School Press.

Lewin, K. (1997) *Resolving social conflicts and field theory in social science*, Washington, DC: American Psychological Association.

Maslow, A. (1970) *Motivation and personality*, New York, NY: Harper and Row.

Mayo, E. (1933) *The human problems of an industrial civilization*, New York, NY: Macmillan.

McGregor, D. (1960) *The human side of the enterprise*, New York, NY: McGraw-Hill.

Mordaunt, J., Paton, R. and Cornforth, C. (2007) 'Beyond non-profit management education: leadership development in a time of blurred boundaries and distributed learning', *Non-profit and Voluntary Sector Quarterly*, vol 36, no 4 (Supplement), pp 148S-162S.

Ouchi, W. (1982) *Theory Z*, New York, NY: Avon Books.

Peters, T. and Waterman, R. (1982) *In search of excellence: Lessons from America's best run companies*, New York, NY: Harper Row.

Senge, P. (1990) *The fifth discipline*, New York, NY: Doubleday.

Taylor, F.W. (1911) *The principles of scientific management*, New York: Harper.

Part Three
Skills in practice

TEN

UK case study

Mandy Young

Introduction

This case study is about Adrenaline Alley, a social enterprise I started and continue to run. The organisation is situated in Corby, a town in the East Midlands of England. It is a deprived town that has in recent years been undergoing considerable regeneration due to it having been categorised as one of the most deprived towns in the UK. Despite its image, however, it is a place I enjoy living in. The focus of the project is urban sports, which are basically skateboarding, skating and BMX riding. In this chapter I describe why I set up the project and reflect on why I choose social enterprise as the particular organisational model.

When I first started this project I had never even heard of the term social enterprises. As will be shown in this chapter my intention in setting up Adrenaline Alley was not to set up a company but 'merely' to set up a project that would help my son and his friends. When I embarked on turning the project into a social enterprise I started to learn about what they were and why, as an organisational form, they were appropriate for the Adrenaline Alley. What you will see in this chapter is the development of a social enterprise that was set up in response to a particular need, a project that was also designed to benefit the surrounding community. You will also see that in order to survive it has had to develop a sustainable business model.

Development of an idea

Before I started the project I had no real idea what urban sports were and never would have envisaged being involved in these sports if it had not been for my son John. In fact I had no idea that urban sports existed until my son met a group of skateboarders and was able for the first time in his life to go out with his peers and socialise. What particularly attracted me to the sports was the attitude of the skaters towards John. John had suffered for 12 years with physical illness and social isolation. He looked thin, yellow, fatigued and was trying to grow his hair after a year of chemotherapy. For John the skaters accepted him for who he was; it was a case of "Respect man, you're on a board!" That was a major step for John in breaking down his personal social barriers.

After a few months of some normality in his life John was attacked by three young people because he had a skateboard. The effect on John, me and the rest of the family was devastating: he did not venture out of the house for a further three years. John continued to skateboard in the garden and his friends would occasionally visit. From contact with John's friends I realised there was a need to provide a place for young people to socialise and build their self-confidence.

Birth of the initial project: Corby Wheels

After consultation with John and his friends a public meeting was set up and I attended under the impression that a few local young people needed somewhere safe to do their sports, naively thinking that a local ramp would be the result. After two meetings it became clear the local urban riders and skaters were passionate and dedicated enough to see the project through to create an indoor park. Corby Wheels Project was born in December 2002.

If the project was going to succeed I needed to undertake research to understand the culture of urban sports and how this idea could develop into a sustainable venture. I also needed to make contact with people in the urban sports industry to attract funding for the future. The more contacts I made the more I realised we had discovered a need that went beyond the local estate and town; it was a national problem. My vision grew to realise that we could provide something really special to become a national exemplar for urban sports and recreation, based in Corby!

What had been crucial in the early stages was the need to consult with the potential users, finding out what they wanted and needed. Growing and nurturing a nucleus of young people helped us all to learn to respect and trust each other; we became a team and the ultimate driving force behind the project. I recognised that because I was not able to skate or ride I needed to connect with the young people, requiring me to listen, watch and educate myself, and that if we were going to take this forward into the public eye together we had to work quickly, loudly, and respectfully and go for the long term. After consultation with the community I realised that attacks such as the one on my son were not unusual, and that as a consequence if I was going to make a difference I would have to galvanise both the neighbourhood and the urban fraternity into action. The need for somewhere safe to ride and skate became a campaign that found supporters in surprising numbers. Aspirations for a few ramps quickly turned into a well-researched opportunity for a fully-fledged indoor skate park.

The lack of a skate park in Corby, as in many other areas nationally, brought about a conflict between local skaters and BMX riders and the general public. The former either had to travel great distances to enjoy their sport, or endure the dangers of riding in the streets and incurring the wrath of the police and owners of the land they skated on. Because of their age and their activity, skaters and BMX riders became scapegoats for vandalism and disturbance and were vulnerable to targeted attacks. The attacks on skaters grew into both local public resentment and a belief that we needed to provide our young people with a safe place to skate and ride.

In the past the UK has seen some successful indoor parks such as Radlands in Northampton, Y2S8 in Peterborough, Derby Storm in Derby as well as numerous smaller outdoor parks situated on local estates. Unfortunately there are few indoor parks left in the UK, many of which are run down and small in comparison to the needs of the participants, therefore they are seen as unsuitable for development of skills or for individual disciplines within the sports.

After a year of voluntary work and research it became clear we were not going to do this on our own. We needed stakeholders from the private and statutory sectors to help us engage the local community and achieve our long-term dream of a safe, indoor park. I initially approached the local council, who politely told me that I did not have a feasible project. I was deflated but at the same time more determined to succeed.

We ruled out local industrial units due to the high monthly repayments. However, in December 2003 we approached the chief executive officer at Rockingham Motor Speedway (RMS) in Corby, who agreed to donate land, pay the overheads and contribute £35,000. The local council later donated £10,000 towards equipment and the Community Safety Partnership set up a two-year agreement to pay for our own transport link for the local community free of charge. Providing something tangible that the young people, who lacked belief in their community, could touch in a short space of time pushed the project to new heights. By July 2004 we had a large outdoor park in a safe environment. It was the biggest outdoor park in the UK and hosted over 13,000 visitors in 20 months.

Developing an indoor arena

The project was developing fast and we were beginning to change community perceptions. People were realising that what we were doing was not only providing an attraction for young people it could also be seen as part of a process of reducing antisocial behaviour and crime in the town. This enabled us to attract funds from the Community Safety Partnership, Local Network Fund, Lloyds TSB, The Tudor Trust and others as we began to be seen to be tackling social issues as part of both local and national regeneration strategies.

Historically urban ramp parks have not succeeded as businesses in the UK. The disciplines within urban culture represent an out-of-control rollercoaster with peaks and troughs that would have been frightening for anyone with a business mind to sustain as an indoor commercial business. From the early 1970s to date there has been no established constructive body or agency in skateboarding, BMX freestyle/street riding and aggressive inline skating to help develop the sports.

During the early period of the project Sport England employed a worker to develop a Community Sports Network and work with local organisations. She brought a strategic perspective, mentoring me to understand how to link local and national strategies into the delivery of the many services and applications that lay ahead of me.

The initial project was located in a lonely temporary building in the middle of an industrial estate. Bigger problems arose in 2005, as it was becoming more evident that an outdoor park was not financially sustainable, because participation was seasonal and began to fluctuate dramatically during the winter months. Against these problems I had to weigh up the benefits, such as the reduction of antisocial behaviour, the numerous activities that were a diversion for many young people, the training and increased opportunities to improve healthier lifestyles and the image we had created as a dedicated and passionate group against the possibility of closure. In my view closure was not an option. I made a decision that it was time to move on and find an indoor venue.

A locally based property developer gave the project new impetus in January 2006 by offering us a 5,000m² former chicken-processing factory on a local industrial estate. When I visited the premises with the community worker from Sport England I was horrified, as the renovation of the property was going to be a huge task and we did not have the expertise or knowledge of how to turn an old freezer/processing plant into an indoor urban centre. After a few weeks of research I decided we had no choice but to risk everything and convince the management committee we had to try and make this work. In March 2006 we signed a five-year lease as trustees of the charity. Although the developer gave us £20,000 towards refurbishment costs, we had very limited funds in place. I immediately set about fundraising, specifically targeting partners we had established to deliver the skate park element of the park as quickly as possible.

Working closely with a consultant, a survey was carried out with both young/old, local/national, novice and professional participants within the BMX, skateboard and inline skating cultures to try and build something for everyone that would help us to sustain the park in the long term. I quickly learned the procedures that I would have to implement to comply with regulations from the local council and with their support managed to implement licences, insurances and policies to the highest standards possible for an urban ramp park. With no secured funding, a group of passionate and dedicated local people had managed to secure £125,000 to prepare and install an indoor park.

Although we were pleased with the work, and the renamed Adrenaline Alley proved popular with the young people, we still were not satisfied. As a result we secured further funds to install the UK's only Resi jump box, a foam pit and bowl that would enable participants whether old or young, novice or professional to train and improve their skills.

Over the last six years I have seen the image of urban sports change drastically, from being seen as antisocial and intimidating to being inspirational and socially accepted. Adrenaline Alley has, I believe, played a key role in that process by demonstrating and identifying the needs of participants and engaging with the community. The incorporation of BMX in the 2008 Olympics has, for instance, added to both the interest in the sport and the need to professionalise the provision.

Marketing the organisation

I had to take a long hard look at my skills and assess my potential to face the challenges ahead. Time was of the essence and I did not have time to study for qualifications. I had to rely on my instinct and common sense. I was good at writing smaller funding applications but was daunted by the prospect of inputs, outputs, outcomes, milestones and impact – what did it all mean? How would I decipher all the information for a project I was not sure I could deliver in the long term? How could I explain my vision so funders would see 'the bigger picture' and understand the value for the community, especially to larger funders when they often required limited wording on applications?

One thing that became apparent from the beginning was getting everyone to understand we were not 'just a skate park'. Although the skate park is our core activity we are a wide and diverse community project. From our consultations we discovered that the vast majority of young people take part in something other than the sport and as a consequence we have developed the project to tap into sub-cultural activities, engaging increasing numbers of young people in activities such as music, graffiti, photography and media workshops.

Engaging so many young people meant we could market the organisation through word of mouth and internet-based social networking sites. To date, we have spent approximately £10,000 over six years on marketing, including our original website design and upgrades. For me, the facility sells itself: make it socially valuable to those who use it, and people will hear about it. We recognise that when we become world class, marketing will be a key factor but until then we continue to reinvest our profits into activities and areas within the venue that are more beneficial to the participants.

I was lucky to have business mentors in the person of the development manager of Social Enterprise for East Midlands (SEEM), the chief executive officer of Rockingham Speedway, and Sport England's community worker, who all instilled confidence in me and encouraged me to "Go for it by doing it". They supported me through knowledge transfer and understood what the funders wanted, the terminology they used and the importance of local and national strategies. I applied to some larger organisations for £30,000-£60,000 and secured all the applications. This was a real boost to my confidence.

Of course, sustainability was an essential aspect of strategic thinking and long-term planning. I needed to prioritise our core activities to generate income. I consulted with participants and to my surprise discovered they "didn't want it to be free". They agreed that young people in society today do not value 'free'. Therefore we came up with an entrance fee structure that enabled young people to access an option membership and provided a session cost from 81 pence per hour to £1.21 per hour, the cheapest of any urban park in the UK. Since August 2006 this has enabled the charity to turn the organisation around from being grant dependent to operational sustainability, and we have employed 15 people.

Revenue funding has always been very difficult to secure, especially in an old chicken-processing plant with a five-year lease. Most funders want at least a 10-year lease and want to measure the impact of funding, but how can you measure the outcomes of paying an electric bill or buying a piece of furniture? Of course, to us it is imperative. Without the funding for these necessities it was very difficult, especially in the early stages of development. We were very lucky that Rockingham Speedway supported us by providing in-kind overhead support and rent/rate free accommodation for the park. In 2006 we were donated the building with local support from the council so became rent and rate free, saving us approximately £200,000 per annum.

Although the current indoor arena has proved very successful, it is not a permanent site, currently still only on a five-year lease. A requirement for our long-term future is the need to build a world-class hub that can co-locate service providers to provide everything under one roof. Luckily capital funding has been available, and in 2008 we secured £100,000 for professional services. By April 2009 we were on track with a comprehensive feasibility study, had submitted a planning application for a four-phase project worth £18.5 million and had identified 12.5 acres of land.

Developing a social enterprise

Our mission has always been to provide a safe and secure environment for young people to participate in urban activities and to be recognised as a leading provider of urban sports in the UK. To ensure this happens, we have used a range of partnerships to become a sustainable social enterprise.

Providing a safe haven where young people could fulfil their potential to achieve personal goals was my aim. Identifying the reason that instilled passion, dedication and drive to progress the project forward came from the heart. Running a social enterprise is not a 9 o'clock to 5 o'clock job and I had to be prepared to do whatever it took to get the project on its feet. Working with young people I quickly recognised that, together with my desire to want to make my community a better place to live and provide better opportunities, we were building confidence, self-esteem and life skills in those individuals, who have provided us with a base to build a crucial nucleus to advance the project.

The urban industry is dominated by males participating in the sports or ex-professionals who have made a living by distributing equipment, so it was going to be particularly hard for me, as a woman, to be taken seriously. Being totally naive about urban sports, I worked hard to understand the culture, image and language used by its participants. The project has engaged over 125 young people playing an active role by organising fundraising and marketing events, researching other parks, the sports and culture and attending training courses. I concentrated on constructing a sustainable organisation by putting in place a committee and ensuring the necessary policies were adhered to, such as child protection, data protection and equal opportunities, and by legally registering the charity and securing funding. I quickly learnt the techniques needed to make a successful funding application while gaining the hands-on management skills to lead the organisation and approach the statutory/private sectors constructively.

In July 2004, I realised that I had provided the young people with something they could call their own and realised that 'ownership' was a powerful and meaningful asset that would become the core priority to prolong their engagement if we were to succeed and become a sustainable social enterprise in the future. What the project had become was not merely an urban sports centre but a place they called their own, and also a place in which young people had the opportunity to gain employment in an area that lacked opportunities.

Local heroes: developing people

A local skateboarder, who joined us as a volunteer, organised RampRock live music events. She got the 'Alley bug' and decided not to return to college to complete her landscape gardening qualification. Her love of the outdoors, young people, the community and urban culture outweighed her gardening passion. In early 2005 she became the assistant manager at the outdoor park and being a small, thin, young female in a male-oriented environment she was not going to find it easy. However, she broke down the social barriers and 'bulldozed' her way to the hearts of participants and stakeholders, working hard to establish her career while gaining the necessary management skills. In 2005, she returned to college to complete her gardening qualification, but in 2006 we employed her again in a role as kitchen manager. She excelled and over two years was promoted to operations manager. In September 2008, she decided to move on and gained training employment working with young people in adventure sports at an activity centre in North Wales, where she remains today and continues to receive awards for her commitment and drive.

In 2004 two young men started with us. They had been subject to targeted attacks or had their equipment stolen because they were hanging about on local streets and BMXing in underground or prohibited areas. On completion of the outdoor park both of them regularly attended the project doing odd jobs and taking part in outreach workshops. They helped out by supporting the bus driver and ensuring there was no unruly behaviour. Over a period of time they demonstrated their eagerness to work and continue their education so we employed them part time. As a result of their involvement they gained essential life skills learning the importance of communication, reliability and team working. In 2009, they secured places at Northampton College and the University of Northampton, enabling them to remain working with us while working towards their higher education qualifications. As well as carrying out park and reception duties, they receive pay incentives to design and prepare all our art work, manage our website and use strategic data to compile statistical evidence to put forward in multimillion pound application forms. They are seen by participants, stakeholders and the Charity as two of the 'faces of the Alley' due to their commitment and long-term loyalty.

To ensure the 'Alley' was not separate from the community we began to engage with more community groups in the arts, music, education and social circles by carrying out workshops to upgrade individual skills. These contacts have helped the development to become a project that is wider than just an urban sports centre, becoming more of a hub of skateboarding, BMXing, street art, music (with the setting up of a studio) and having an educational unit attached. The young people take pride in the project, showing respect for each other and the centre; to date we have not had to exclude one person. The project has increased the confidence and skills of the young people and for the wider community has provided young people with a place to go in a town that does not have either a cinema or bowling alley.

Private sector involvement

During the first six months of operation the development manager for SEEM introduced himself because he recognised the social value the project was delivering. This was the first time I had ever come across the idea of a social enterprise. His mentoring skills and knowledge of running social enterprises helped me to identify and improve the organisation, secure major funds, increase individual skills and use all that education to drive the charity forward and keep it on a sound financial footing. He is now vice chair and a trustee.

Trading as a social enterprise means long unsociable hours, initially with limited resources, often working to the demands and needs of others. As we began to raise our profile and be taken more seriously I needed to get private sector sponsorship from a reputable company. I approached the managing director of the largest company in the town, who was direct, blunt and sceptical: "You must be joking! Come back when you are serious and have something more tangible. You will never be able to deliver such a big project."

After six months I returned to the same company and presented a copy of annual accounts to the managing director and showed him that I had exceeded all the targets I set; I was targeting more community, school and youth groups and therefore increasing and improving participation, with 13,000 individual young people using the project in 18 months. He was amazed, we had won his respect and he could see that the impact of the project was rippling out through the community. We began a working partnership that continues to flourish today. The company continues to be a key stakeholder contributing to our success and is a major investor in Adrenaline Alley. The managing director has retired from the company but remains as chair and trustee of our enterprise.

"Challenge the Alley"

It is important to stress that although we are dependent on funding from outside sources the project would not survive on grants alone. We are a trading company with customers who have to pay to use the facilities; we have a differential charging policy with members being charged lower rates. We also have a shop for equipment and a café that sells healthy snacks. It must be remembered that although I set up the project to address a particular need it has to be run as a business if it is to remain viable. The social mission of the 'Alley' is clearly interconnected with a sustainable business model; the two cannot be disconnected.

Adrenaline Alley has since grown rapidly as a project and is now well established in the former chicken-processing factory. Between August 2006 and June 2009, over 18,500 people have used the facilities in over 80,000 visits. The boarders, bikers and skaters are mostly aged eight to 21 and they stay for anything from three to nine hours at a time. We have secured over £1 million in funding that includes service level agreements, local authority agreements, private/public sector funding, grants and in-kind contributions.

Working with partners such as Northamptonshire Enterprise Ltd has helped us to understand the wider benefits such as the economic value we contribute to local businesses. Because of the equipment we have and the fact that BMX racing is now an Olympic sport, for example, we have attracted people from other parts of the UK as well as Europe, providing significant benefit to the local bed and breakfast hotels.

Conclusion: the future

We were able to access capital funding to undertake a comprehensive feasibility study identifying the need to progress to a purpose-built world-class facility and the further potential to develop a model that can be franchised to other areas to create smaller 'little Alleys' to develop safe, organised and effective facilities benefiting young people and investors such as borough councils and the urban industry itself. Although each community's needs are different, we can use our knowledge and business model to help other interested groups to work with their local communities to set up similar projects focusing on both the social values and the business approach to set up a sustainable operation.

Securing funding has never been easy, despite the success of the project, and one of the lessons I have learned is that securing funding for the everyday running of the project is sometimes much more difficult than securing funding for a capital project. Becoming a social entrepreneur has undoubtedly helped me to recognise my individual skills, upgrade them and pull together my past work experience skills. I believe that social entrepreneurs are pioneering innovative individuals who want to help people. My experience of working in the urban sports culture has shown that many people involved in the sports (particularly young people) are dyslexic, have poor academic attainment and are numerically and literacy dependent on those around them. I believe the Alley is a national exemplar of how a grass-roots project can develop into a sustainable large business while keeping its core objective at the heart of the business. This has been recognised by a number of awards.

We will continue to develop the project, responding to community need and also using the sporting focus to develop nationally recognised coaching qualifications and a wheeled urban sports association. Opportunities to continue expanding boundaries into new and unique projects through education, business and social activities will have lasting national benefits for individuals, companies, professionals and novices throughout our area. Unique partnerships are forming with educational providers, training organisations, businesses and youth organisations, including the Youth Offending Team.

Organisations such as Adrenaline Alley are traditionally known as third sector businesses. As more individuals and organisations aim to tackle social issues, there is increasing interest in organisations which combine social missions with corporate methods. Social enterprises are becoming more recognised for their passion to 'get on with it' without the bureaucratic approach of always having to 'dot the Is and cross the Ts'. Above all, the passion, dedication and social value running as a common thread through Adrenaline Alley has been my inspiration to continue working to make a difference to my community and to everyone who participates.

ELEVEN

US case study

Kimberly Sugden and Anthony Mendes

Historical and contemporary context for social entrepreneurship in the US

Throughout the world, millions of organisations provide services to address social problems that affect billions of people. Many of these organisations are non-governmental organisations (NGOs), civil society organisations (CSOs) and other types of non-profit agencies that have specific missions and approaches to solving the ills of society. In the US alone, the social sector consists of 1.5 million organisations, with annual revenues over US$700 billion (Wei-Skillern et al, 2007).

One thing the majority of these organisations have in common is the on-going challenge to provide ever-increasing demand for services with dwindling financial resources. To deal with this dilemma, many organisations are turning to innovative ways of increasing revenue, through earned income initiatives, and creative solutions to secure resources through non-traditional means. The term often used to describe this innovative approach is social entrepreneurship. While there are numerous descriptions and definitions for social entrepreneurship, it is most commonly viewed as 'the pursuit of opportunity beyond the tangible resources that you currently control', (Stevenson, 1983 p 131). In this definition, opportunity is any activity requiring the investment of resources in hopes of a return on these investments (Wei-Skillern et al, 2007). The return, with non-profit organisations, is expanded or improved services to those in need.

Opportunities are more than just great new ideas. They are carefully assessed and evaluated initiatives that have potential to improve efficiency and delivery of services. Opportunities for traditional or commercial entrepreneurship are often found in at least three distinct areas, including technological innovation, political and policy changes and social or demographic changes. Opportunity recognition includes the ability to look through a different lens at familiar issues. Brainstorming processes with customers, employees, stakeholders and sometimes competitors can bring new opportunities into view. Thinking differently and incorporating the perspective of others can be threatening to existing processes and approaches; however, opportunity exploitation often requires giving up or abandoning programmes that are not resulting in more effective and efficient ways of providing service.

While social entrepreneurs look to these three areas for new opportunities, they also explore mechanisms that successful entrepreneurs use to produce revenue that involve earning it in the commercial marketplace through the sale of products and services. The major challenge to social agency leaders with this 'entrepreneurial' approach is maintaining the mission and purpose of the organisation while initiating profit-seeking programmes.

Characteristics and traits of successful entrepreneurs have been studied extensively in the US and other countries and societies throughout the world. Common characteristics of entrepreneurs include need for achievement, risk taking, desire for independence and extroversion (Shane, 2003). Entrepreneurs are also individuals who have a high 'internal locus of control', which is the belief that they have control over their environment, and 'self-efficacy', a compelling belief in one's ability to perform a given task.

Entrepreneurs also have a strong will and ability to follow through and deliver on objectives, especially in challenging and trying times. The view of entrepreneurs as careless risk takers is a misconception. In fact entrepreneurs are very good at calculating risk and determining the best alternative to competing options. The difference is that entrepreneurs have a 'higher tolerance' for risk and are able to pursue uncharted territory without clearly guaranteed outcomes. Social entrepreneurs are also able to take advantage of unplanned incidents and the potential opportunity inherent in them. For example, natural disasters and political change can create unanticipated opportunities and resources that rarely come along. The key is an ability to respond quickly to these opportunities and not be mired by administrative or bureaucratic processes.

Another area in which social entrepreneurs seem to excel is in utilising social networks for information and securing other resources in exploiting opportunities. Expanding networks, by joining organisations relevant to important issues they are pursuing, is another characteristic of social entrepreneurship. Networking, in the traditional sense, is not new to leaders of social organisations; however, strategic alliance and leveraging of resources is a cornerstone for developing entrepreneurial initiative. This ability becomes more relevant in light of the current global economic challenges, where scarce financial and human resources are increasingly difficult to come by. Effective networking utilises new technology-supported systems for networking, such as Facebook and LinkedIn, as well as the ability to bring in individuals who have specific skills not currently available to the organisation. Social entrepreneurs also rely on volunteers with diverse skills to provide a wide range of functions from board advisers to daily tasks required to deliver services. In order to attract highly talented volunteers, social entrepreneurs must be creative in providing rewards and incentives that do not correspond to traditional methods found in for-profit organisations.

The value base for social enterprise formation

Over the past two decades, non-profit agencies have been pursuing income-earning strategies at an increasing rate. In the US, it has been estimated that earned income was the largest growing revenue source for non-profits in the 1980s and early 1990s (Salamon, 1997). While many social agency directors want to be viewed as creative and resourceful in developing programmes, there is also additional pressure being applied from outside funding agencies and boards of directors to develop income strategies. The primary goal of any programme to increase revenue should be to strengthen the mission of the agency, not merely produce income. In fact, the most successful income-generating strategies of social agencies are those that build on the primary strengths and assets of the organisation. The three main strategies for income generation are:

- getting paid for products and services the agency provides that are aligned with the organisation's mission;
- launching a new venture that may or may not be associated with the core mission of the organisation;
- income strategies that create revenue streams that appeal to the connection purchasers have with the mission of the agency.

The third type of earned income may include cause-related marketing, through which products or services are marketed by associating them with a particular agency or cause. This could involve licensing agreements through which a social agency allows its logo to be used by a business company in marketing and sales of products.

Social enterprise case study: The Enterprising Kitchen

An entrepreneurial spark can generate a life-changing idea at any given moment. For social advocate Joan Pikas the inspiration to provide meaningful life skills training to women developed from years of working as a social worker. But in 1995, as Joan was counselling women in uptown Chicago, and teaching a Graduate Equivalency Diploma (GED) class in Evanston, she began to notice that just life skills training by itself wasn't very effective; attendance in her classes was irregular and women were dropping out of the programme. Joan could see that the women were enthusiastic about learning, developing life skills, and receiving mental health counselling, so what was the powerful external factor keeping them from attending class and keeping appointments?

Identifying a social need

After having heart-to-heart conversations with several of the women, Joan discovered that their class and counselling absences occurred on days when they were offered external opportunities to make money. Nearly all of these women came from low-income households, where they were the sole provider for their families. But most importantly, work ensured that food would be on the table and children would not go hungry. Joan discusses her entrepreneurial idea to add employment to social work training, and the immediate need it filled for many women: "What I saw was how much more important it was for these women to have employment. They didn't really see that they themselves had any value, even though they had skills. That revelation really inspired me to figure out how to combine, education, training, and employment, and after doing research, I happened on to Women's Bean Project, another social enterprise company, and I had a model to go by and an inspiration for The Enterprising Kitchen."

Founding of the company

In 1996, Joan founded The Enterprising Kitchen (TEK), a non-profit social enterprise in Chicago, Illinois, to provide workforce and life skills development to unemployed and underemployed women. The goal of Joan's new company was to combine both short-term employment with training/education modules, to build self-esteem and prepare women for sustainable full-time jobs. Providing income to the participants of The Enterprising Kitchen helped build a stable and reliable base for the women and allowed them to concentrate on developmental learning and future goals.

Joan's first operational decision was to identify a product that The Enterprising Kitchen could undertake to make money. This activity had to be something that the women could make by hand in their small start-up facility in Chicago. Joan wanted to replicate the successful impact realised by the Women's Bean Project, thus The Enterprising Kitchen began by packaging food under the name Gourmet Grains. Joan talks about the company's immediate impact: "When we started out with Gourmet Grains it quickly became obvious that just working with your hands and making something was very empowering. And I had, almost from the very beginning, women saying to me 'I didn't know that I could work ... I didn't really think I could do this and get paid and I feel so good about myself.' It was almost immediate gratification, even though there were a lot of women who couldn't make it, their history of drug abuse or other issues kept pushing them back. But even still, I know that we made a difference in their lives and probably those of their extended family."

Entrepreneurial spirit and determination

Four women participants were selected out of Joan's existing counselling groups and production was under way until one day, when disaster struck. "We had just really gotten started in our first year, we had rented a space and we had been there for a couple of months and there was a huge fire in the building in the early morning. Our office was up on the third floor, and the whole third floor of the building was destroyed." Joan recalls that terrifying morning: "Cathy, my co-founder, called me, hysterical, at quarter to seven in the morning, saying turn on the news, The Enterprising Kitchen is over, you won't believe it. Cathy's initial reaction was we're done for – that is it." But Joan's entrepreneurial spirit would not let her give up on The Enterprising Kitchen so quickly. "Yes our product and records were burned, and our four women participants had basically scattered, but I went out to round them up. My first reaction was, we need to stay strong, get off the phone and get down there to get on the news; we had to make people know what had happened."

The building had housed a number of other social enterprise companies, and as Joan rushed to the scene she was met by several founders who were all searching for interim office space to rebuild from the ashes. "It was an epiphany for me that Cathy's reaction and my reaction were so very different," Joan comments. "But The Enterprising Kitchen did go on! We went out and rounded up the women participants, and found some space in the bottom of a church for a brief period of time that we could use." Joan's ability to mobilise the limited resources she could find as quickly as possible unified TEK and put the company back in business despite their tragedy. Joan remembers leaning on volunteers for support and help: "Eventually, one of the volunteers that had been working to help us recover, ultimately found the manufacturing space that The Enterprising Kitchen ultimately rented, which was home up until two years ago when we moved over to the larger Ravenswood location."

Changing times and challenges – product development – the switch to soap

Rebuilt from the ashes, Joan was determined to deliver on the mission of The Enterprising Kitchen and to help more women. But manufacturing of food products continued to be more difficult than previously anticipated, as product shelf-life had to be closely monitored for spoilage, and product placement in grocery stores proved very costly. The grain products were not selling very well, so Joan enlisted the help of a team of graduate students, whose feasibility study revealed that the company would have far greater success selling gift items. "I was really struggling at the time thinking how are we going to keep these women busy," Joan commented. "In talking to an acquaintance I was telling her about this dilemma and she said make soap, which I had no idea how to do. She told me 'it's so easy Joan, go get a book,' and I did." Armed with a recipe book and the determination to seize this new opportunity for growth, Joan took a risk and experimented with soap making. She found the process to be very efficient and easy to teach the women, but would consumers buy this new product?

The strategic decision was made to manufacture soap and spa products from only all-natural ingredients to tie into the company's holistic vision for adding comfort and well-being to life. Suppliers were chosen very carefully to ensure purity and quality of ingredients, fair supply pricing, and variety and uniqueness of scents and oils.

The Enterprising Kitchen's product line began simply, with bars of cold-process soap of various sizes, scents, and colours. Over the next few years, clear glycerine soap, liquid hand soap, and shower gels were added, followed by bath salts, candles, and bath teas. In 2005, the company was looking to add additional value to their product offering, and expanded into gift basket production to meet customers' suggestions and generate significant revenue with minimal additional cost.

Custom products

The Chicagoland market provided The Enterprising Kitchen with a variety of custom-branding opportunities and partnerships with corporations and other social ventures. Bars of soap are the most requested custom items because companies want gift items, and logos and custom scents can easily be added to the tailored product.

The Chicago Shedd Aquarium has been a long-standing collaborator with The Enterprising Kitchen. From its early years, board members from both organisations had utilised networking and product exchanges as a way to build awareness for each others' brands. Lynne Cunningham, executive director of TEK, explains the creativity of a current project that was designed exclusively for the Shedd Aquarium: "The custom product is a bar of cold-processed soap that's been coloured in a pale blue and will be stamped with the logo of the Shedd Aquarium's capital campaign theme, titled 'Scrub the Tub.' These will be given to a range of donors."

Employing and educating women in need

TEK's dedication to training and empowering unemployed and lower income women is at the heart of their social service mission and is the core driver behind their diverse educational programmes and mentoring. In 2007 TEK was able to help 69 women throughout the course of the year, and in fiscal 2008 was able to educate 40 new participants. Women stay at TEK between six and 12 months, until they can find a permanent job or continue their education, to graduate out of the programme.

All of the women participants are single, and most are also over 30 with families to support. The workday hours were strategically selected to run Monday through Thursday from 9:00am to 2:45pm, so that women would have enough time to arrange childcare, run household errands, attend job interviews, and fight child custody hearings if needed. Education is very important, and most women come with either a GED or high-school equivalent.

Selection of participants

Women participants are all referred to TEK from a range of different organisations depending on the timing of recruitment campaigns. Lynne explains, "They are organisations that tend to work exclusively with women, some of them are supportive housing organisations, some of them are organisations that have a mission to deal with ex-offenders, some are rehab centres. We also work with the Cook Country Sheriff's department."

During its early years The Enterprising Kitchen also worked with agencies, like Apna Ghar, Asian Human Services, even Heartland Alliance in Chicago, which took in immigrant and refugee women. Joan remembers the desperation of many of these participants: "Some of these women were brought to this country by their husbands and then abandoned or abused. Whether they were from India or Pakistan or Thailand, if their husbands left them, often they couldn't go back to their countries because their families for cultural reasons wouldn't have them back. I had many women tell me that divorce was worse than death, as far as they were concerned, because they had nothing. Many of them had never been educated and they were desperate and destitute."

Joan fondly remembers the impact TEK made on a participant from Turkey, who had been referred from a social services organisation: "She unfortunately had been a victim of domestic violence, and had come to us with basically no papers in order, but she very much wanted to work and needed anonymity because of her abusive husband who she was trying to get away from. She is a very smart woman, who had been professionally trained in chemistry and had worked as a pharmacist back in Turkey. She successfully came through the programme, and has actually been with TEK for seven years. She now serves as the chief soap maker member of staff, and is a wonderful inspiration and mentor to new participants."

Joan was very proud of the international aspect of the workforce programme and had a large map in the office representing every country where women participants had originated. She comments that having such a globally diverse group of women added a rich depth to the social training experience at TEK: "There are many stories like that of our chief soap maker, and I think that having such a mix of women at The Enterprising Kitchen, is a real learning process. Women see that their problems, as awful as they may seem, are no worse or better or easier than the person sitting next to them, who maybe came from Africa and maybe spent their whole life in a refugee camp."

Application and rotational programme

All applicants must go through an interview process, where they are asked about their life ambitions, educational and work experience backgrounds, skills/qualifications, and what type of jobs they enjoy. The management team then looks to identify traits in the women that fit needs on the production floor or call centre, so they can best pair participants with fulfilling work. TEK does have requirements that all women must meet, explains Lynne: "We are not taking women who have a retail theft background, no violent crime, no possession with intent to deliver. If someone is coming to us with a background in substance abuse they have to be in recovery for at least four months, and we're really pushing for it to be longer. If they are coming to us from a housing programme, they need to be in transitional housing, not emergency shelters. And they have to have a willingness to go through the training programme."

Participants begin the work training programme by stepping through a rotational programme that includes direct sales/marketing, customer service, manufacturing, shipping/logistics, and assembly line production. This experiential learning opportunity helps participants see first-hand the challenges and issues that need to be overcome on a day-to-day basis when running a company and taking ownership for work produced.

Addressing the need for educational components

Life skills education has been the core mission of The Enterprising Kitchen since its founding. All TEK women participants step through a structured life skills workshop series, taught by Bob Perkins, a retired Chicago case manager. He emphasised the development of personal self-esteem and self-awareness as the cornerstone of long-term fulfilment and success. The course has been nicknamed 'How to go along and get along' because of its truly transformational impact for individuals and their surrounding personal connections.

When participants begin their self-awareness journey by first recognising their unique skills and strengths, they not only transform themselves, but they affect friends, family, and co-workers around them. Lynne Cunningham talks about why a programme like this is necessary to achieve a long-term impact for TEK participants: "I'm not sure that when the women come to us they know to look for that, but it is a reflection of the situation that they come from and how they handle themselves in that situation. So the programme is actually driven by us saying that those are the behaviours we're seeing on the floor that need to be addressed if women are to be successful when they leave here." Customisation of life skills learning is critical to ensure that the social needs of all the participants are being met. If TEK management sees reoccurring interpersonal issues that should be addressed, the incidents are used as examples in workshops to open dialogue and showcase different positive ways of addressing social solutions.

All TEK participants also take a personal financial literacy course that walks through bill payment, savings techniques, loan acquisition, tips for running a household, and other basic financial strategies. Additionally, women who need computer skills for their future careers are offered a computer training course, so that they can showcase defined technology proficiency on their resumé and during job interviews. The Enterprising Kitchen has also hired private tutors to work with women who want to pass their GED test.

Further education is also offered through a therapy group to women who have been victims of domestic abuse. Participants have found great comfort in talking through their emotions and being surrounded by caring and loving women who understand their feelings and questions.

Participants also learn invaluable lessons from one-to-one mentoring that happens on the TEK floor every day. Informal mentoring between participants, TEK staff, and volunteers is inspirational to everyone and forms lasting impressions and memories. In particular, one volunteer at TEK is making a real impact, discusses Lynne: "We have one volunteer who is a manager at Banana Republic, who has really taken to our women, as our women have taken to her. She is very involved in so many wonderful ways. The best thing is that volunteers can help with any role at TEK. If a volunteer calls and says they want to help, we have them come in, take the tour and we chat about what they like to do, what we need to have done, and we see if there is a match."

Career placement

Women from TEK tend to go into helping professions. Many graduates have worked as successful substance abuse councillors, nurses, and elder care professionals. Of those women that graduate, 100% are placed in either jobs or schooling. Furthermore, of the women that begin full-time jobs, on average, a tremendous 70% are still employed a year after graduating from the programme.

From education to career placement, Lynne explains the career process and why it is so critical for continued success: "What we're doing right now, is we help women prepare a resumé based on their past work experience or life experience. And then at some point during the six months, the employment manager will start to help them discern more about what they want to do and then actually help them look for jobs. Our employment manager will also help them go through a mock interview, to make sure they are ready to go."

The women also help each other talk through misconceptions about interviews and job applications. They share many stories about difficult questions that were asked during interviews, good answers and information to cover with employers, resumé tips, and rumours about which companies are good to work for.

Marketing and branding

In 2003, The Enterprising Kitchen undertook a major rebranding campaign of its product line and image, as the company looked to strategically move into increasingly upscale markets including specialty boutiques, custom corporate orders, and incentive products. The early soaps had embraced a 'down home natural' aesthetic with its green packaging colour scheme, and had simply been called The Enterprising Kitchen Soaps.

Stakeholder expertise and brand creation

Kari Ness Reidel, a bright graduate student from Northwestern University, who had served as a TEK volunteer and board member, was approached by management to create a brand identity. Joan was confident that Kari's marketing expertise and intimate knowledge of the TEK mission and products would result in a new image that resonated with the heart of the company. TEK was able to network with Kari's full-time employer, Monitor Consulting Group, who signed a philanthropic agreement and lent Kari to TEK for four months while paying the majority of her salary. Joan remembers the critical importance of the rebranding campaign: "Kari was the one that came up with the brand identity, Choices from The Enterprising Kitchen®. It was just a perfect name, because we were really trying to talk to the women and teach them this all the time; we always tried to help them make better choices in their life, while also hopefully teaching consumers to make better choices in their purchases."

To complement the new branding, TEK turned to another key stakeholder, board member Kris Clemons, co-founder of Gerhardt & Clemons marketing and design firm. Kris's company was able to very economically design a new aesthetically clean label with modern complementary background colours that were utilised for product labels and bags and integrated a thin, contemporary, all-capitals font.

Directors specifically targeted the incentive market as having the largest sales growth potential for long-term sustainability of the TEK product line. The owner of Hinda Incentives created a specific collaborative called Helping Hands Rewards to bring together a socially responsible product line that companies could incorporate into their incentive programmes. He was eager to include The Enterprising Kitchen because of the real impact product sales made on the lives of the women participants. The incentives industry promised to give TEK increased brand exposure through their catalogues, as thousands of corporations used incentive programmes to reward their employees and customers.

Remaining mission driven

Emotional attachment to the brand

Perhaps the most popular and unique feature on The Enterprising Kitchen's product labels is the inclusion of the mission statement and a signature from one of the women participants. Customers deeply identify these two pieces of branding with the social causes TEK stands for. Even back when the company was Gourmet Grains, management knew that the personalised touch was a great marketing tool. Joan Pikas specifically remembers one customer call from the early days: "We had people calling us and saying, 'Well I bought these black beans that were made by Sue, is she still there?'"

TEK management also utilised the labels to bring women participants closer to the mission of the company and to feel a part of a real community. The signature tags often became a moment of inspiration and pride for the participants, as all women signed products, no matter what their involvement with the production line. Lynne provides a perfect example of how integral the label is to each product: "This morning when we were hosting a private party, we had a couple of products that didn't have all the labels on them because they had just been made. People were specifically asking for the labels and other materials that they could pass out with the products."

Balancing the mission and the business

It can often be difficult to find the perfect balance between wanting to increase sales using sound business practices and meeting the social mission of The Enterprising Kitchen. Management must continually look towards generating growth for the company, to make a greater social impact.

A good example of this balance can be seen within TEK's most famous and popular signature product, the 'soap on a rope', which is constructed by tying colourful pieces of remnant soap together. Joan explains how the company wanted to be economical to reduce discarded soap trimmings and product error: "Soap on a rope was generated from the lot of waste, as we would cut something wrong or make it the wrong colour. Initially we were trying to make soap balls with our waste, but that was getting very labour intensive."

Instead women hand carve these remnant pieces into shapes and letters that have various fragrant scents and stunning colouring, and tie them together on a string to make beautiful potpourri. "That is very empowering because there are so many creative women out there, and they have a chance to make their own designs," comments Joan, while also noting that creativity and business need to work in harmony. "You have to keep in mind that doing things like this is expensive because people get side-tracked; they are really involved in making their pretty flower or whatever soap on a rope shape they are working on, but on the other side, you are trying to run a business and you need some efficiency and it's costing you money. There can be a real tension there."

Creative funding to build sustainability

Funding growth

The Enterprising Kitchen has seen steady financial growth since 1996. Joan recalls the early years and the company's seed capital: "In the beginning, Cathy and I didn't take a salary. We just did a lot of grant writing and once we got our first $10,000 grant, from the Frye Foundation that was funding start-ups, we had everything lined up; we knew what our product was going to be, we had interviewed women, and we were ready to start the business. Once we had that first grant then others quickly followed. And then we also started asking for donations from friends and family, and we got some large gifts and were off and running."

Sales drive social benefit

The financial sustainability of the workforce development programme is driven in part by The Enterprising Kitchen's soap and spa product manufacturing. Since 100% of sales go back into the business, the number of women participants that TEK can bring on is directly correlated to how profitable the company is and if sales are increasing or declining. Throughout TEK's history, Joan recalls positive sales trends: "The portion of the operating budget that was supported by revenues from product sales increased steadily over the years. When we started out, it was 20%, then 25%, and we were so excited when it was 30%, then it got up to 50%, and in 2007 it was over 50% and growing."

Networking to build resources

Joan networked closely with corporate contacts to increase sales, and in 2004 her hard work paid off, and a large promotional gift order from the Quill Corporation rocketed sales and the brand reputation of The Enterprising Kitchen to new levels. "We were on a big learning curve because it involved having to work with complicated packaging for fork-lift warehouse trucks, and stringent measurements and weight specifications," Joan comments. "It was lots and lots of products, a huge order for us. We visited Quill headquarters and they gave us a $10,000 gift in addition to the merchandise order. I remember being so impressed when I went to the office because they had the whole story of the family business and its growth on the wall. I was really impressed by their entrepreneurial dedication, and very interested in sharing our story with their generous management team."

In addition to product sales, The Enterprising Kitchen utilises fundraising as another core component in their financial model. Every April, The Enterprising Kitchen throws its large fundraiser, lovingly named The Bubble Bash. The event is driven by the support and time donations of dedicated volunteers that serve on the TEK Board of Directors and people from the community who want to help. Items from the silent auction, live auction, and raffle bring in money to fund women participants and operations for the following fiscal year.

The Bubble Bash also brings a wide range of corporate sponsorship and networking opportunities with companies in the Chicago area. The Lyric Opera of Chicago is an excellent example of an organisation that collaborates with TEK to exchange donation gifts, helping to promote both organisations, while standing in partnership for the greater social good.

Conclusion

Most of the challenges faced by The Enterprising Kitchen are ongoing, as management looks to expand their product line, help more women participants, and increase their brand awareness. Over 265 women have graduated from The Enterprising Kitchen, and the lasting impact on their lives and families is immeasurable.

Joan Pikas reflects on her journey as a social entrepreneur and the women her venture has forever changed: "My whole reason for doing TEK is that it is so satisfying. That sounds selfish, and I guess in a way it is, but I have always been about helping these women so that their lives can get better." Joan's words ring true of the thousands of social entrepreneurs in the US that put their company mission and values before money, prestige, and purely business objectives.

The determination to face challenges, coupled with the ability to recognise opportunities and mobilise resources is at the heart of any great social venture. The Enterprising Kitchen is a testament to overcoming adversity and rising out of the ashes to eternally impact lives. Much careful planning was needed, but as Joan points out, sometimes luck and risk taking plays a large role: "It is so amazing that the soap turned out to be this great thing; but anyone can make soap. What makes TEK stand apart is that this manufacturing business is making a difference in these women's lives. There are tensions between running a business and being an agency that is really about providing service. My heart has always been with the women and being able to make a difference; the business didn't come first, so it doesn't matter if you're making soap or candles, it's about changing lives. My interest both for The Enterprising Kitchen and my new social venture, Bright Endeavors, is let's make this business work so we can be able to keep more women coming and having these great experiences. I always said we don't employ people to make soap; we make soap to employ people."

Evaluation of the current state of social enterprise and its vision for the future

While still in its infancy, social entrepreneurship has taken hold in the US. In higher educational institutions there has been an expansion of new courses, degree programmes, and numerous experiential learning opportunities for students interested in social enterprise. There is also a growing interest among not-for-profit organisations to incorporate entrepreneurial concepts and educational opportunities in their organisations.

The intersection of educational initiatives with community organisations provides an added dimension of interaction with students, faculty, and community agency leaders. These growing collaborations help existing social enterprises expand quickly and strategically, while presenting young academics with inspirational models for success of their own social ventures in the future.

Additionally, in the US the term 'serial entrepreneur' is used frequently to highlight the determination and drive of many social venture entrepreneurs. These individuals are known for their innovative founding of several companies and their ability to take risks and learn from business mistakes. Serial entrepreneurs are growing in number, as enterprising individuals recognise the opportunity to apply lessons learned from their first businesses to help additional groups of people in need. In fact, many of these successful serial entrepreneurs are investing their time, money, and entrepreneurial talent into forming new socially focused entrepreneurial foundations that help create sustainable and highly effective change in social agencies.

References

Salamon, L. (1997) *Holding the center: America's nonprofit sector at a crossroads*, New York, NY: Cummings Foundation.

Shane, S. (2003) *A general theory of entrepreneurship: The individual – opportunity nexus*, Cheltenham: Edward Elgar.

Stevenson, H. H. (1983) 'A perspective on entrepreneurship', *Harvard Business School Working Paper*, no 9-384-131.

Wei–Skillern, J., Austin, J., Leonard, H. and Stevenson, H. (2007) *Entrepreneurship in the social sector*, Los Angeles, CA: Sage.

Website resources

Ashoka: Innovators for the Public 2007, Ashoka, Arlington, VA: www.ashoka.org

Echoing Green, Echoing Green homepage, New York, NY: www.echoinggreen.org

Global Social Benefit Incubator 2009, Santa Clara University, CA: www.scu.edu/sts/gsbi

Skoll Foundation 2003-2009: Social Edge, Palo Alto, CA: www.socialedge.org

Skoll Foundation 2009: Skoll Foundation, Palo Alto, CA: www.skollfoundation.org

Social Enterprise Knowledge Network (SEKN): http://sekn.org/en/index.html

Social Entrepreneurship at Change.org, San Francisco, CA: http://socialentrepreneurship. change.org

The Enterprising Kitchen, Chicago, IL: www.theenterprisingkitchen.org

Tides Foundation 2009, San Francisco, CA: www.tidesfoundation.org

University Network for Social Entrepreneurship, www.universitynetwork.org

TWELVE

China case study

Marie Tze Kwan So and Carol Chyau

Introduction

Historical and contemporary context

There is a need to solve China's social problems in a more innovative and sustainable manner. While the economy on the eastern coast is booming, serious social ills are exacerbated by widening income inequality, environmental degradation and loss of social safety net. Despite the rising inequality, international development organisations are cutting their budget for China projects or pulling out because they believe that the Chinese government now has the financial resources to solve its own social problems.

In China, the number of people living on less than US$1.25 a day in 2005 was 207 million. Resources and innovation are needed to bring development to marginalised communities in an efficient and sustainable manner. Since innovation and energy lies within the vibrant private sector, we believed that if we could direct some of the entrepreneurial energy and resources from the private sector towards solving social ills, we could develop truly innovative and home-grown approaches of social entrepreneurship which could achieve development.

Social enterprise landscape in Greater China

While social enterprises are playing a greater role in many other countries, they have yet to develop in China (see **Table 12.1**). Here social entrepreneurship is still at its infant stages, mainly due to the following binding constraints:

- poor understanding of the concept
- lack of home-grown examples.

Table 12.1: Analysis of social enterprise (SE) development in China

Symptoms	Why	Root cause	Intervention needed
Most people do not understand the concept of a for-profit business that aims to solve social ills	The model is significantly different from traditional concepts of philanthropy. Non-profits have always been dependent on grants and donor funding rather than generating their own funding through a business model	Non-profits have a hard time understanding the concept of SE because it challenges their traditional mindset	Non-profits need to be educated and challenged through analysing both local and international case studies of SE
People are unwilling to experiment with actually building a social enterprise	There are not enough cases or track records of successful portfolios. Given that this sector is so new, the risk is very high. Few donors are willing to financially support risky ventures in the social arena	The barrier to entry for developing SEs is high because there is limited funding that gives room for experimentation	Providing funding not just to ripe ideas, but to ideas that still require pilot testing will lower the barrier to entry
Current examples of SE are primarily one time projects of non-profits or activities of for-profits that are trying to revamp their social image	They are trying to build SEs without changing their organisational structure and mental model. Overhauling traditional ways of thinking and innovating requires too much effort	It is hard for current non-profits and for-profits to start SEs without changing their original mental and organisational structure model	Organisations need to concretely see how SE is a superior way to their current model in order to have the motivation to create change within their organisation
Many are attending workshops and trainings of SE, but few are following through to implement	The gap between hearing or learning about the concept and actually implementing it is too large. People lack the experience and skills sets to move from ADOPTION to ACTION	Although people are interested and attending workshops, they lack adequate support to actually implement their ideas	Leading potential social entrepreneurs through a step-by-step process will increase the number of people who are willing to implement SEs

Existing players can be divided into four categories, namely social venture funds, network and resource platforms, academia and social entrepreneurs. Most organisations work on promoting awareness. The Hong Kong Council of Social Service, Social Enterprise Resource Centre creates a platform and provides resources to support the growth of social entrepreneurs; the Hong Kong University Social Enterprise Incubation Centre and Hong Kong Social Enterprise Business

Plan Competition generates awareness by analysing overseas cases; Social Venture Fund (Hong Kong) and Flow (Taiwan) provides starting up funding and technical support.

Most organisations in the Greater China region are promoting the growth of social enterprise by generating awareness through organising workshops and conferences or providing funding. The challenge is that with social enterprise being such a new concept, going to a workshop without adequate support follow-up is not enough to encourage an aspiring entrepreneur to take action. Given the lack of aspiring social entrepreneurs with adequate skills sets, few projects are ready to be funded. For others who have started implementing social entrepreneurial ideas, their work has remained on a project level rather developing into a full-blown enterprise.

Most non-profit organisations in the region are volunteer-based, government run, or religiously affiliated. Several local non-profits in the region have developed social enterprises under their umbrella organisations as one-time ad hoc projects. However, they are often trapped by the need to pursue grant money provided by government or social welfare instead of building sustainable long-term goals for the development of social enterprises in the region. Other non-profits focusing on the same issue have not adopted the hands-on approach because it requires the implementing team to have the long-term commitment to actually start a social enterprise. It is also easier to raise funds, organise workshops, and provide short-term technical assistance. On the enterprise level, non-profits have not launched social enterprises because of their organisational structure, expectations of donors or skill set of employees, but because they are more geared towards grant-dependent projects such as building schools and medical centres.

Ventures in Development: an introduction

The Ventures in Development model

Ventures in Development (VID) is a non-profit that strives to be a catalyst in the creation of more social enterprises in Greater China. We define social enterprises as for-profit businesses that explicitly aim to achieve both financial return and development impact. Given that the basic needs of society are met, we believe that promoting the growth of social enterprises is a more sustainable way to achieve higher levels of economic and social development. Our mission is to identify, incubate, and implement ideas that have the potential to become sustainable business enterprises that yield quantifiable direct social benefits (see Table 12.2). The idea of promoting social entrepreneurship by itself is not innovative, but our approach is. Our theory of change is that to promote the growth of social entrepreneurship, we must work through the dynamic growth process of first action, then awareness, and finally adoption. By first taking ACTION to implement our own social enterprises, we are able to use them as home-grown case studies to generate AWARENESS. Through the experiences that we have accumulated, we then have the credibility and expertise to coach other aspiring social entrepreneurs to ADOPT their own ideas.

Table 12.2: VID enterprise development model

Identify	Incubate	Implement	Pilot	Scale up/spin off
Identify development-based and market-based opportunities	Conduct rigorous market and industry research. Develop business plan	Launch pilot project to test feasibility of the concept	Expand the pilot into a full-blown for-profit business	Invite investors for capital to grow and scale up

VID history

In 2005, while at Harvard University in Cambridge, Massachusetts, the two of us (Carol and Marie) discovered that we shared the common belief that social enterprise could possibly achieve development in a faster and more innovative way than traditional ways of approaching development, and that we both wanted to experiment with this in Greater China. Greater China was our target location in part because, with one of us from Hong Kong and the other from Taiwan, Greater China is our home. It is where we feel a strong sense of duty and commitment.

In early January 2006, we travelled to Yunnan Province, Western China to test the feasibility of our concept by sharing our ideas with local non-profit organisations and government officials. From our field trip we gained further understanding of the needs in different communities and identified one abundant yet underutilised local resource – yaks. We started our social enterprise adventure by leveraging China's 13 million yaks to generate broader economic impact for Tibetan communities. Between finishing up our coursework and writing our Master's theses, we spent most of our waking moments researching and writing business plans for yak cheese and yak fibre. We took numerous field trips, from visiting fibre farms in Connecticut, to familiarise ourselves with the textile process, to cheese farm hopping in Vermont to understand the cottage cheese farm industry. Ideas from the initial discovery trip were crystallised through participating in various competitions in the Harvard Community including the annual Social Enterprise Track of the Harvard Business School Business Plan Competition and the global Business in Development (BID) competition. The competitions encouraged us to keep going forward and provided initial funding for us to pilot the ideas.

Ventures in Development was established in March 2006 in the US *and* registered in Hong Kong in January 2007. Shokay was established September 2006 with expanding business registration and operations in China starting 2007. It has focused primarily on two ideas, both of which are separate for-profit enterprises: Shokay, and Mei Xiang Yak Cheese. Both projects seek to develop unique products for the high-end international market by utilising one abundant resource in Western China: yaks. In Shokay, we ourselves are the social entrepreneurs, using soft yak down collected from fibre cooperatives in Qinghai to develop luxury textile products for the fashion industry. In Mei Xiang Yak Cheese, VID uses immediate and hands-on experience from Shokay to provide technical expertise to a Tibetan family in Yunnan to develop, distribute and market gourmet yak cheese. For both social enterprises, herders with greater income will have the means to reach the end: choice. They will have the opportunity to send their children to school, and to seek proper medical and health care, and at the same time maintain their tradition of yak herding for many more years to come.

While social enterprises may be a possible solution, among both the public and private sector there is still very little understanding of the concept and few home-grown examples in China. Hence the need for our organisation to develop successful case studies and provide the platform to incubate more innovative ideas (see **Table 12.2**).

Case study I: Mei Xiang Yak Cheese

Identifying need and business opportunity

Yunnan Province, located in the most south-westerly part of China, is endowed with rich natural resources, vast biodiversity and a diverse culture. Highlighted in all travel books on China as a must-see destination, the province encompasses an area of 394,000 square kilometres, bordering neighbours Laos, Myanmar and Vietnam. Out of China's 56 recognised minority populations, 25 are found in Yunnan.

Jeffrey Sachs, author of *The end of poverty*, has long argued that geography is the root cause of poverty (Sachs, 2005). Geographically isolated from large market towns, many of these small rural villages remain poor because people lack market information and the necessary infrastructure to develop human, physical and financial capital.

Langdu Village of Geza Township in rural Yunnan, home to 112 Tibetan families, is one such example. An expanse of rolling mountain tops, Langdu derived its name from the familiar presence of a yellow flower distinct to Shangri-la. In Tibetan, *lang-du* means 'poisonous', as the flower carries toxic chemicals used by local Tibetans to make traditional herbal medicine. The ancient existence of Langdu flowers is strongly reminiscent of Tibet's extensive history in the region and of the people's traditional values and lifestyle. However, the villagers there struggle to survive at subsistence level, with annual household incomes of only US$320. They also have very limited access to education, infrastructure and health care.

Of the population, 80% are semi-nomadic, having on average 30 yaks per family. Wealth is measured by the size of their herds. Herders live in the villages during the harsh winter months, and raise their yaks on the remote mountaintops during the spring to summer months. Yaks are the lifeline of Tibetan people. Their outer guard hairs are used to make waterproof tents and ropes; their soft inner down is used to make clothing and blankets; their milk is made into solid yak yogurt (*nai zha*) and yak butter (*su you*); and their backs are used to carry heavy items. Most of the yak bi-products are only used for individual household consumption, in part because there is limited market demand for these products, and in part due to geographic isolation. Although Langdu is only 85 kilometres away from Shangri-la, the journey can take up to six hours due to the poor road conditions.

As much as geography is a constraint to development in areas like Langdu, so is trade. Another camp of development practitioners believe that more important than geography, the integration of trade and access to market is the key driver of economic growth (Frankel and Romer, 1996). Although our team could not change the geographically isolated situation of Langdu, we knew we could help create better access to markets.

When our team first visited Yunnan, we were captivated by the abundance of natural beauty – blue skies, luscious fields and mountain ranges that stretched across the horizon. These rich natural resources are not fully utilised. In addition, Northern Yunnan averages about 3,000 metres above sea level, the harsh climate making development a challenging feat. While tourism is generating economic development in certain areas, it is encroaching on traditional lifestyles at an alarming rate, with only a handful of individuals benefiting from the industry.

Stakeholder participation

Yaks are abundant local resources and Tibetans have been dependent on yak dairy products for centuries. Developing gourmet yak cheese suitable to the western palate would not only create an economic opportunity without changing herders' traditional lifestyle, but would also generate long-term social impact for them. Professor Ranee May, Professor of Dairy Sciences from The University of Wisconsin-River Falls, visited the cheese farm in 2006 to teach the Tibetans how to make a western-style cheese using yaks' milk. The native Langdu cheese-making family, led by head cheese maker Lu Rong Zhuo Ma and her Aunt, Sang Ji Zhuo Ma, learned and worked hard. In just two years they had started a cheese factory using their own resources. The cheese farm is named Mei Xiang Cheese Farm (美香奶酪廠). Mei (美), to represent the technical skills they learnt from the US experts and Xiang (香) to signify that they are from Shangri-la. If their cheese farm were successful, not only would it provide greater income for the family, it would also provide a sustainable income for the local community by sourcing milk from the herders in the villages.

While there are many local herders in the region, initially few were willing to participate because they did not want to follow the stringent sanitation procedures required. They could not understand how there might be a greater market for yaks' milk outside of Yunnan, and certainly not for yak cheese. However, through a series of local village meetings, the cheese makers were able to convince 12 families to supply high-quality milk. The next challenge was the collection of milk. Yaks' milk is only available during summer, which is also when the Tibetans herd their yaks to the tops of neighbouring mountains for fresh grass and wild flowers. At an altitude of 4,000 metres, with only a few families living on each mountain top, accessibility to their homes is a challenge. In order to maintain the freshness of the milk, the cheese makers tried to minimise herders' travel time by setting up a collection point at the base of two adjoining mountains. Still, some herders have to hike for two hours with milk canisters strapped to their backs before reaching the collection point. For the first two years, the Mei Xiang Cheese Project remained in its early growth phase. Despite the leadership and passion of the entrepreneurial Tibetan family, growth was limited because with little information about the outside world, they did not know how to enter the market.

Knowing that we could assist the Tibetan family to develop new skills and access the market, our team entered the project in 2006 working with them at the cheese farm. Professor Ranee May introduced new cheese-making techniques and sanitation procedures, assisting the cheese makers to pass international food and hygiene standards. Our team learned alongside the Tibetan family everything from dairy production to health and hygiene, as well as sanitary dairy processes. In the mornings, we oversaw the milk collection process at the herders' huts, sanitising the milk production equipment and testing the milk. In the afternoons, we made fresh cheese. We also provided the financial resources to upgrade the farm from a small log cabin to a fully-fledged cheese farm that could meet international standards. When the new farm was completed, we developed a system to efficiently manage the milk collection and cheese production schedules; to forecast sales, develop marketing materials, and measure sustainable development impact. Our team also guided the entrepreneurial family to develop a business plan, and equipped them with the appropriate business skills and knowledge so that one day they could manage the farm independent of outside assistance.

Introducing yak cheese to an international palate

When we first started this business, we were warned of the difficulties of working in the food industry in rural areas. Yet we entered the project precisely because of this challenge. Our goal was to create a market for an abundant, but underutilised local resource – yak milk. We wanted to give yak cheese a legitimate place in the gourmet western cheese palate. Moreover, we wanted to show that rural entrepreneurship in remote areas can be possible, and integration with the outside world can still occur despite geographic isolation. If the Mei Xiang Cheese Farm is successful, the pilot would open possibilities of replicating cottage cheese farms in Shangri-la.

In fact, not all dairy farms on the plateau need an international market for yak cheese. Villages along the road from Nagchu to Lhasa, for example, have set up businesses that sell traditional yak yogurt to passers-by with the assistance of the local government. Since many Tibetans living in Lhasa do not have herds of their own, there is strong local demand for traditional yak dairy products. In Yunnan, however, because most Tibetans in the region have their own herd, they can make their own yak products rather than purchase them from the market. Hence producing a western-style gourmet cheese palatable to western tastes would create a higher value-added product with a different market.

We first introduced our cheese to the western audience in the autumn of 2006 at a tasting hosted by the Beijing Cheese Society. We served two types of cheese: Shangri-la Premier, which is modelled after Halloumi, a fresh cheese used in salads, sandwiches, or fried, that is often found in the Mediterranean area; and Geza Gold, a cheese modelled after an aged Asiago, which has a stronger flavour due to the two-month minimum ageing process. Our cheeses received much positive feedback and enthusiastic support.

In summer 2007, we assisted the family in setting up The Shangri-la Yak Cheese Shop, which is the first yak cheese shop in China. Located in the Old Town of Shangri-la, the cheese shop serves hot sandwiches to hungry tourists, cheese and crackers to hikers who want to pack a snack, and sells to expatriates in the region who crave the taste of real cheese. The shop also helps service high-end hotels like the Banyan Tree and local restaurants that use the cheese in their cheese platter and own recipes. In December 2007, the cheese officially passed international food safety standards. This was a significant milestone. It was the ticket to accessing the international market. In January 2008, Mei Xiang started to distribute its cheese to the Hong Kong market.

2007 was a year of many challenges, from building the new factory to exporting the cheese. 2008 - a year of scaling up the operations; the factory will need to produce 12 tons of cheese to meet market demand. This will mean training more herders for sufficient milk supply and therefore this translates into increased income for more herders in the region. In 2007, the incomes of the participating herders have increased threefold. In 2008 and 2009, we have expanded herder household participation by 15% with a threefold increase in income. Currently we own two retail shops in Shanghai and are looking for further expansions in 2010.

Case study 2: Shokay

Identifying need and business opportunity

While learning about yaks for the cheese project, we discovered that the animal also has a soft-downy fibre comparable to cashmere. Tibetans have always used yak hair to make tents, ropes, blankets, and clothing. If yak down can keep people warm in the bitter climate of the mountain ranges, it must have unique properties. The question then is why is it an unknown material in the market?

We devoted our last semester at Harvard studying yak fibre. We scoured all possible resources and purchased every sample we could find. Initially, we only came across blends that had less than 10% of yak fibre. So when we dug our fingers into 100% pure yak down for the very first time from a small bag of fibre shipped to our Boston apartment from China, we bubbled over in excitement.

To compensate for our lack of knowledge of the fibre and textiles industry, we, as Professor Jeffrey Silberman, assistant chair of the Department of Textile Development and Marketing, puts it, "parachuted into his office" at New York's Fashion Institute of Technology (FIT) to seek expert advice to develop a business strategy. With slivers of yak fibre, we visited designers, yarn spinning farms, and yarn stores to gather market information and consumer feedback.

On graduating in 2006, we trekked across China to visit universities, research institutes, textiles manufacturers, development organisations, government agencies and local Tibetan communities. We wanted to test the feasibility of our concept on the ground. The journey led us to Hebei, Gansu, Qinghai, Yunnan, Sichuan, Tibet and Inner Mongolia. We tracked down Dr Han Jianlin, a leading yak expert, who then connected us with most of China's yak experts.

Through our investigation, we discovered that yak down is truly a luxurious and unique fibre still relatively unused in the fashion world. Each yak produces about 0.5 kg of fine downy fibre. The average fineness of down from an adult yak is 14-20 microns, while the length is around 30-45 mm. Yaks that live in higher altitudes have finer fibre. The most common natural colour of the yak is a dark chocolate brown, but can also be found in white, tan and grey. Unlike wool, the scales of yak fibre are in a waved mosaic pattern, resulting in a very smooth fibre that does not itch. We discovered also that the absence of this unique fibre in the fashion market has largely to do with its geographic isolation. Since 80% of the world's yak population is on the Tibetan plateau, it has been largely shielded from the fashion world. Manufacturers in China have little incentive to develop the fibre because there is no demand for it; fashion brands have not been using it because their suppliers have not introduced them to the yak down fabric. Our discovery of the potential of yak fibre led us to building our own social enterprise, Shokay. Our value proposition is to introduce an exotic, affordable luxury product with socially conscious origins to the consumers. Shokay is 'luxury with a story, style with a touch of humanity'.

Working with our fibre cooperative in Qinghai

To find a starting site for Shokay, we analysed locations across the Tibetan plateau by conducting detailed studies of regional and local demographics, as well as economic and social variables to find an ideal site to set up our first fibre cooperative. Our basic criteria were Gross Domestic Product (GDP) per capita, amount of yaks in the region and access to transport. Our research led us to set up our first site in Hei Ma He Township, located in the Hainan Prefecture of Qinghai province. Qinghai, a region of plateaus with an average elevation over 3,500 metres above sea level, is also the source of China's three great rivers: Huang He, Yangtze and Mekong. Qinghai is famous for Qinghai Lake, the largest salt lake in China. For centuries, pilgrims have been walking around the sacred lake for blessings, and more recently, cyclists have joined the route.

Hei Ma He Township, located at the far corners of Qinghai Lake, is a four hour drive away from Xining, the provincial capital of Qinghai. The township is divided into four villages and has a total population of 14,000. Our first pilot site is Zheng Que Hu Village (ZQH). Here, 291 households struggle to survive with an annual per capita income of only RMB 3,400 (renminbi, people's currency, or yuan). Most villagers are Tibetan nomadic herders of the Yellow Sect, living in flat brick and mud houses in the winter and yak hair tents in the summer. There are around 45,000 livestock in the village, of which 8,040 are yaks. Each family has on average 30-40 yaks and relies primarily on livestock, collecting caterpillar fungus and other short-term jobs for income.

In the past, Muslim traders had come by to purchase fibre at a low price. Our concept was to train the herders to comb higher quality yak down so that we could pay higher prices for the fibre. By sourcing directly and cutting out the middlemen, we would help increase their income based on their existing assets – yaks – to create higher value-added products.

When we first approached the village, apart from government-appointed positions, there were no other structures within the local economy to govern trade or markets. Given the lack of a formal institutional environment, we organised the herders into local cooperatives, divided each village into subgroups and appointed villagers as 'Shokay representatives' to mobilise their communities. By building cooperatives and formalising a market structure, we hope to build local capacity from collective bargaining to accessing the market.

Working in ZQH village is no easy feat; as any development practitioner in the field would say, "On a third best day, something might work." The theories and methodologies that we had learned were very different when trying to put them into practice. Best practices from foreign countries also might not apply in China. Despite our good intentions, we still had to build trust and relationships with local government, village heads and villagers. Most have had negative experiences with fibre traders and other non-profit organisations that work in the region. As we worked with the cooperatives, we also collected demographic data through lengthy meetings with each household. The meetings provided us with data to do need assessment and run impact evaluations, but also gave us an opportunity to understand and learn about each other. Beyond setting up logistics and operations for fibre sourcing, we had to work with yak experts from the Qinghai Bureau of Animal Husbandry to train herders on how to best extract fibre from combing specific body parts of the yak. Every grade of fibre commands a different price to encourage herders to comb the highest quality fibre and hand sort only the finest down.

Bringing Shokay to the world market

As industry novices, we experienced a lot of 'learning by doing'. Everything was 'our first time', from working with communities collecting fibre, managing the manufacturing process, choosing fabrics, designing knitwear, to launching a new retail brand. In autumn 2006, we launched knitting yarn, scarves and throws. Sales and feedback from our first winter season were encouraging. People loved the quality of the material and the meaning behind it. In 2007, we expanded our lines to include a fully developed Home, Accessories and Kids Collection. To support our production, we organised a hand knitting cooperative on Chong Ming Island near Shanghai. Chong Ming Island is an agricultural society with highly skilled hand knitting labourers who were trained in neighbouring key textile manufacturing cities such as Ningbo and Suzhou. This gave us another opportunity to provide employment in rural areas. The knitters work on customised orders and each individual piece is stamped with the name of the knitter to create a completely personalised Shokay experience.

With our newly developed products, we entered the international market by participating in multiple tradeshows. Promoting Shokay is not easy, as most people are unfamiliar with yaks. Those who are familiar with them, consider yak down to be an inferior, rough and smelly fibre; that is, until they touch and feel our products. We were under a lot of pressure to do well; if our products were not well received, not only would we miss sales targets on the business end, but we would also miss our development objectives of direct income generation for our herders.

The Shokay Yarns and Shokay Collection of Home, Accessories and Kids are now carried in over 150 stores, from Hong Kong, China, Taiwan to the US, Europe and Japan. The market has been very receptive to our product, in part due to the exotic appeal and the quality of the fibre; in part because it fits the current trend of cause-related marketing and going green. Between Bono's RED campaign and the increasing usage of organic cotton, it is now mainstream to be socially minded. Many companies are now using corporate social responsibility as an opportunity to enhance their company image and media coverage. We are one step ahead of them; creating social impact is not an afterthought, but a core component of our business model. Our story gives us a marketing advantage, but at the point of purchase, quality and design of the product are still more important.

As more people experience the warmth and softness of the products, we will be able to engage more communities, build more fibre cooperatives and widen development impact along the Tibetan plateau. With greater income, the herders will have the *choice* to self invest in areas such as health and education.

Key learning

Are the rural Tibetan communities in Yunnan and Qinghai poor because of low productivity in an unfavourable geographic location, or because they are relatively isolated communities with limited trade from the outside world, or because they lack the necessary institutions to create functional markets? In theory, we need to target the root causes of poverty instead of the symptoms. Despite our time spent in the region, we have yet to find the right answer.

First, we hypothesise that rural communities in Yunnan and Qinghai are poor because of geography. In addition, there is little integration – the world outside is unknown to them, and they are unknown to the world. While geography cannot be changed, integration can. In both of our enterprises, Mei Xiang Cheese Farm and Shokay, we are seeking to build bridges from these remote communities to the outside world through trade. Rather than grants, subsidies, or cash hands-outs, we give the herders cash in exchange for raw material that can be developed into luxury products. We are innovatively trying to create a new market for products that people did not previously value. We are not extracting diamonds because we know the market will pay a high price for them; we are finding rocks that we think can be refined into gems. In addition, in both cases, we have begun to build local institutions through our dairy and fibre cooperatives. By establishing rules for the cooperatives, we are helping to create a functional market. Is it geography, trade, or institutions? Perhaps at different stages of development, each factor takes on a different level of importance.

Through these two businesses, we have had to wrestle deeply with many issues in this newly developing sector. For example, we wanted to measure social impact through the double bottom line, meeting financial and social sustainability objectives. We have collected detailed demographic data through household surveys for each of our participating households so that in a few years we can rigorously measure whether we have truly made an impact. We believed in 'development as freedom', but freedom is intangible. We can only estimate whether we have helped our communities achieve a greater degree of freedom through traditional indicators such as an increase in income. How does one take the intangible social impacts into account while trying to quantitatively calculate the final dollar value of a social enterprise? Valuing the social enterprise is important because we must analyse whether the final output was worth the initial input, and whether our model was truly able to solve a social ill in a more efficient and sustainable manner.

Other issues we have run into include:

- balancing the delicate trade-off between financial return and social impact;
- finding the most effective and transparent way to govern social enterprises;
- sharing profit between investors, entrepreneurs, and community.

We learned that entrepreneurship begins with passion and innovation, but can only be sustained through perseverance. It is at the same time more challenging than we had ever imagined, but also more exhilarating. Professor Heifetz, our leadership professor at Harvard University, always reminded us to "periodically stand on the balcony and observe the dance floor". With our heads so often buried in the technicalities of our work, from time to time we have to force ourselves to think at the macro level and focus on the big picture before diving back down again to micro level execution.

Social enterprise is not the only way to achieve development, nor is it an easier way, but it is definitely a way that deserves further exploration. When people ask us why we chose this career or how we stumbled across the idea of championing yak products with so little known about the product and the market, we nod in agreement that this is definitely a road less travelled. Chasing yaks was never in our plans when we prepared for our education at Harvard, nor was it anticipated from our professors who were training us to be practitioners for the World Bank, the United Nations, or national policy makers. If we had not made such choices, we would always wonder about the 'what if' and the 'what could have been'. We would never have heard of yaks, or learned that they grunt; never have started Ventures in Development, peddled cheese across China, launched our own luxury fibre line, or earned our rights to be 'the yak girls'. And we certainly would not be able to tell our story now with a glass of wine and slice of yak cheese in hand, while snuggled underneath the warmth of our 100% yak throw!

Conclusion: envisioning the future

VID's vision is to provide an innovative platform for passionate individuals to encourage social entrepreneurs in the China region. Over time, we also hope to develop a deeper understanding of the various grey areas of this field, such as balancing the potential trade-offs between business and development; conducting fair valuations on social enterprises; determining the best governance structure for SEs; how governments can provide a better institutional environment.

We hope to bridge the gap between the private and public sector. On the side of the private sector, we hope to encourage more business leaders to consider how they can shape their businesses to solve social ills. On the side of the public sector, we hope to increase the degree of professionalism and encourage more non-profits to implement projects that have potential to be financially sustainable rather than grant dependent. Given that both business and development skills are needed to run social enterprises, it would also encourage more people in the non-profit sector to seek out business experience and more people in the business sector to consider how they can use their expertise in the social arena. As more people take action to create successful social enterprises, more people at the grass-roots level would be able to benefit from the innovations made towards solving their social problems.

In a society where the civil sector is run by volunteers, untrained personnel, and religious organisations, we show that it is possible to build a professional career on cutting edge philanthropy. Because we began developing our idea while we were still students and launched it after graduation, we show that if you find the right idea and have the passion, courage, and perseverance to pursue it, it is possible to create something from scratch. We hope to generate awareness and inspiration among the younger generation.

References

Frankel, J. and Romer, D. (1996) 'Trade and growth: an empirical investigation,' *NBER Working Papers* 5476, Cambridge, MA: National Bureau of Economic Research, Inc.

Sachs, J. (2005) *The end of poverty: Economic possibilities for our time*, New York: Penguin Books.

THIRTEEN

India case study

Stan Thekaekara

Introduction

Historical background

The year is 1974. I am a fresh college graduate from South India. The early seventies were the years of student power – the civil rights movement in the US, the student revolution in France. Those were heady times. India was not left untouched. It was difficult to be a concerned university student and not be radicalised.

I was no exception. My years at university had been marked more by the time spent in what used to be called 'extra-curricular activities' and less by the time spent in the classroom. Being president of a National Catholic Student Movement dominated. We huddled around coffee and discussed Marx and Paulo Freire late into the night. For every perceived injustice we would march the streets with hand-drawn placards and shout ourselves hoarse. We took part in work camps in villages where we helped build schools or irrigation canals. But late at night, with blistered hands and aching bodies we would analyse why these people were so poor. Why were we so privileged? A statistic that had been drilled into our heads was that only one of every 1,000 students who enrolled in school made it to college. Each of us was one of those thousands. In the village we would see children who had barely had a year of schooling. The injustice of it got to us, and we vowed we would change the world. At a student convention in 1972 in Poonamallee outside Madras, we signed the Poonamallee Declaration where we ended with the pledge: "We were born into an unjust society and we are determined not to leave it as we found it!"

In 1974, at 21, I marched off into a small Adivasi (indigenous people) village in Bihar, North India, armed with little else than a smattering of Marxian analysis and Liberation theology from South America, determined to bring about the revolution which we believed was just around the corner.

As I write this in 2009, it is almost 40 years since that day – and the revolution has not happened, at least not the way we thought it would. But we are still fighting for social justice. Doing different things at different times, trying to keep pace with the changes in society, to ensure that the voice of those who are deprived gets heard, that they continue to claim their right to a share of India's growing wealth. Over the years different badges have been stuck on our lapels in an attempt to define us – troublemakers and radicals, social action groups, social activists, community organisers, non-governmental organisation (NGO) leaders, development professionals, and, more recently, social entrepreneurs.

It is interesting that each decade appears to be different. The 1970s were the period of mass mobilisation for social justice. The focus was on the root causes of poverty – exploitation, inequality and injustice. The problem was structural and systemic.

In 1977, a gigantic tidal wave and cyclone of tsunami proportions destroyed the eastern coast of Andhra Pradesh. International aid agencies flocked to India in response, bringing financial and other resources to help ease the trauma of the disaster. It attracted a new generation of young people who came as volunteers to help. For many it was a life-changing experience. Tapping into these international resources they set up organisations that worked on long-term development programmes for the tidal wave affected villages. This spread to other parts of the country. But to attract these resources one had to be legally registered, be more structured and this laid the foundation for a very different type of intervention in the 1980s.

The 1980s saw the emergence of a plethora of NGOs across the country. Many social action groups morphed into NGOs. This was fuelled by the government of India recognising the role of NGOs in poverty reduction and allocating budgets to support them. Working for the poor now became socially acceptable. It was no longer the realm of die-hard leftist radicals. Middle-class professionals who do not necessarily have a political or social justice vision, but who, for differing reasons, are unhappy with either the private or public sector, are now attracted to this third sector. And so the 1980s came to be the decade of development professionals.

In 1991, the government of India, under pressure from the World Bank and the International Monetary Fund, went down the path of structural adjustment and opened up its economy. Liberalisation was the word used for what was essentially an opening up of markets for foreign direct investment – creating new opportunities for western capital to invest. With this, markets began to dominate the economy and the causes of poverty shifted from being local and national to global. Those of us who were working for and with the poor suddenly found ourselves having to deal with markets, not something we knew much about. It signified a shift from exploitative landlords, and unjust government policies to the more amorphous notion of 'market forces'. It is during this period we see, not just in India, but across the globe, the emergence of market-based interventions to tackle poverty, Fairtrade being one of the best known.

The 1990s also saw new entrepreneurial approaches in business, creating wealth for some. This triggered the thinking that using entrepreneurial solutions to tackle social problems was the need of the century. Many successful business entrepreneurs started putting their money behind this new model – creating private foundations that backed individuals who appeared to have an entrepreneurial social idea. This dominance of market-based approaches was the springboard for yet another set of actors emerging on the horizon of social change, social entrepreneurs.

So over the last few decades there have been different approaches to social change. These can be categorised as the Social Activist Approach dominant in the 1970s, the Development Approach of the 1980s and the Social Entrepreneurship Approach that emerged in the late 1990s and grew to prominence in the new millennium. The differences between these approaches is characterised by the funding, the type of people involved and the nature of their activity. This is shown in **Table 13.1**.

Table 13.1: The different approaches to social change

	Social activist approach	Development approach	Social entrepreneurship approach
Funding	Small budgets, mainly to cover living costs and travel	Large budgets for not only programme and capital costs but overheads as well	Large budgets but less dependent on grant money and more dependent on capital investments
People	Committed passionate catalysts	Professional, such as doctors, educationists, managers etc	More business- and management-oriented professionals
Nature of work	Mainly mass mobilisation in one form or another – highly focused on rights and justice	More focused on improving quality of life through delivery of services like health and education and income generation	More focused on markets and finance

So what works best?

In order to choose what works best we must first be clear about the values that drive us. If what we seek is to ease the pain of the poor, the developmental approach is perhaps the most attractive. If it is to create innovative solutions in a market to increase incomes and benefit for the poor then the social entrepreneurship approach has relevance. But if we are driven by a desire to go beyond all this and transform society itself, to create a just and humane society, the luxury of an either/or choice evades us. We need an approach that embraces all three – the passion, commitment and mass mobilisation capabilities of the social activist, the resources and managerial skills of the development professional and the market savvy, creative and innovative ideas of the social entrepreneur.

This chapter is about this kind of social entrepreneurship – the kind that tries to bring about social justice. Entrepreneurs are those who create value (Dees, 1998). With business entrepreneurs this value is measured almost solely by the wealth created. For the social entrepreneur, while wealth creation may be important, it is not central. What yardstick can then be used to measure the value creation of the social entrepreneur?

Given the political background in which my work is rooted, I would argue that social injustice stems from unequal power relationships and that therefore the 'value creation' can be measured through the creation of power for the powerless. Just as the creation of wealth is the framework in which business entrepreneurs operate, the framework for social entrepreneurship will therefore be empowerment.

How does the creation of power take place? From our combined experiences of 30 years of working with communities, my wife and I conclude that for greatest impact it is necessary to combine the different approaches of social justice, development and social entrepreneurship. This is especially crucial if one is aiming for sustainable, irreversible systemic change that not only creates opportunities for communities to move out of poverty and provide a dignified, decent life for their families but also bring about social change. It is through the combined creation of **political power** – the ability to influence policy decisions that affect their lives; **economic power**, which reduces their dependence on more powerful sections of society for their livelihoods; and **social power**, which enables them to achieve standards of living that are comparable with those around them; that we can hope to see true and lasting social change.

It is this kind of thinking that has driven us over the years to embrace all the approaches – not by shedding one cloak and donning another but ensuring that even as we adopt a new approach, the value with which we began is woven into it.

It is against this background that Just Change was launched (www.justchangeindia.com; www.justchangeuk.org) – a radical new trading and market system that links producers, consumers and investors in a cooperative relationship. Just Change seeks to maximise the benefits for those who until now remained on the fringes and were often victims of the rampaging juggernaut of the market economy.

Just Change: a case study

This case study describes a full-blooded market-based intervention that grew out of a purely political intervention to assert the rights of a completely marginalised community in South India. As it moved through the different stages of social activism, developmental programmes and market-based entrepreneurship, it has remained true to its roots of social justice action and its mission of bringing about social justice.

The origins of Just Change

The activist phase

Just Change has its roots in ACCORD (see www.adivasi.net), founded in 1986 to work with the Adivasi people of Tamilnadu, South India. These simple, peaceful and dignified people, dependent on the forest and the land for their livelihood, had been reduced to being daily wage earners, many as bonded labourers working on land that was once their own.

The main aim of ACCORD was to correct a historical wrong by mobilising the community to reclaim their ancestral land – to ensure that they could participate in society as equal partners on their own terms and in dignity and pride. All we needed was a small committed team and just enough resources to support them. Support from friends and a small grant from a Dutch donor agency got us started. Village level organisations called Sangams were formed, which federated into the Adivasi Munnetra Sangam (AMS), and a massive Adivasi land rights campaign was launched

The development phase

Soon we realised that taking the land back was not enough. The Adivasi did not have title and so needed to secure it with a permanent crop as evidence of their possession. Tea was the crop of choice. As we went from village to village we realised that health was a very serious problem. People were not accessing any kind of modern health care and infant and maternal mortality was above the national average. We decided to act, so we launched a community health programme where women from the villages were trained as health workers doing frontline preventive work. Over the years our involvement in health care has grown into a comprehensive health care system which includes a 20 bedded hospital (see www.ashwini.org).

There was yet another critical problem – hardly any of the children were going to school. Sitting in a classroom for the entire day was an alien concept for these children. So we started *balwadis* or pre-schools to get them used to the notion of school. This grew into a large education programme that includes village level schools as well as a central school and teacher training centre (see www. vidyodaya.org). This phase took us down the path of more mainstream NGO development work. But this meant we needed large-scale funding – almost 100 times the annual budget of the activist phase. We also needed professionals such as doctors, accountants and educationists.

By the mid 1990s the AMS had grown into a 2,000 family strong community organisation. It controlled a number of satellite community organisations that provide basic services to their community. Nearly every family had a steady independent source of income, infant and maternal mortality had fallen well below the national average, and more than 97% of the children were going to school and, more importantly, staying in school.

At another level the world was changing. Globalisation and free market capitalism was taking control and its impact could be felt even in small remote village economies like ours. The most palpable impact was a crash in tea prices. Our initial hope that eventually the Adivasis would earn enough from their tea to be able to pay for the services being provided now seemed highly unlikely as their real incomes were rapidly decreasing. All the ground gained over two decades appeared under threat.

The market economy phase

During the mid 1990s, even before tea prices crashed, we realised that our tea-planting programme had catapulted the Adivasis from a local wage economy into a global market economy. While we had broken their dependence on their exploitative non-Adivasi neighbours, we had made them dependent on unseen 'market forces'. Local non-Adivasis were quick to capitalise on this and stepped in to market the tea produced by the Adivasis. Where they once exploited their labour they now exploited the Adivasis by cheating on the weight and prices of their produce. New forms of vulnerability had emerged.

Our immediate response came in the form of two interventions. The first was to develop a strong collective economic base to bolster the individual family economy. This was going back to the traditional Adivasi economy based on common property resources. In the modern economic context a tea and coffee plantation seemed to be the answer. But this meant serious money: over 20 million rupees (or a quarter of a million pounds sterling), which was nearly five times our then annual budget. As expected, traditional donor organisations turned us down – they had not yet caught up with the changes in the economy and were still only prepared to fund the more typical developmental programmes related to health and education. We approached banks but the repayment terms were not feasible. Finally help came from an unexpected quarter. An independent charity in the UK – the Charities Advisory Trust (www.charitiesadvisorytrust.co.uk) came forward with a loan. And so we bought the Madhuvana Plantation – a 176 acre tea and coffee estate.

The other intervention was the setting up of the Adivasi Tea Leaf Marketing Society. This was a cooperative that bought the green leaves from the Adivasi farmers and sold it to the factories. We suddenly became a major supplier of tea, giving us far more bargaining power to negotiate better prices. Further, this enabled us to eliminate the middle men.

It was at this stage that the real impact of globalisation hit us. Tea prices tumbled and these market-based interventions seemed under threat of collapse. We looked around for solutions and came across fair trade. It seemed the answer. GEPA, a fair trade wholesaler from Germany, agreed to buy our tea and Adivasi tea soon hit the shelves of German One World shops. But we were quick to realise the limitations of fair trade. One was that they could only take a small fraction of our produce. The premium earned when spread over our entire produce was negligible. Secondly, and more importantly, was something that occurred to us when a group of Adivasis visited Germany. They were moved to happy tears at the solidarity and warmth of the fair trade community, but were puzzled by one thing. Bomman the secretary of the AMS voiced this when he declared: "These people are paying more for our tea. This is not FAIR, they are our friends – they should pay less for our tea!" Bomman brought a completely new dimension into market economies – that human relationships can influence market decisions.

Subsequently, my wife and I visited the UK at the invitation of the Charities Advisory Trust and the Directory of Social Change to look at northern poverty from a southern perspective (Thekaekara and Thekaekara, 1995). On this trip we visited a number of deprived areas in the UK and found poor people drinking huge quantities of tea. Not for them fair trade – they could not afford the premium. But these people were as much victims of the system as our Adivasis were. They were our natural allies. Surely if anyone should be drinking our tea – it should be them! Why don't we develop marketing links that could reach our tea directly to such communities both in India and in the UK? So the idea of Just Change was born!

Just Change: the theoretical framework

Beyond income generation

Traditionally, development organisations have looked at economic development to alleviate poverty through the narrow lens of income generation. This linear single dimension analysis of poverty led to the conclusion that poverty can be reduced by merely increasing people's incomes. Things are no longer that simple. We now live in a world of interconnected economies and we need to look at the economies of poor communities from a more holistic perspective and not just from the perspective of increasing incomes. We need to analyse where this increased income goes and who really benefits?

The Just Change concept seeks to go beyond income generation by first ensuring that people's incomes flow back into the local economy as much as possible thus having a multiplier effect, and second, if it must flow out, to ensure that it flows, as much as possible, to other similar communities rather than into the 'market'.

Beyond fair trade

Isn't this what fair trade seeks to do – source directly from producers and ensure that they get a fair price for their produce by passing on the fair trade premium to them? Yes, but Just Change seeks to go beyond that. First it would like to make it possible for poor and disadvantaged consumers to participate in the fair trade movement. But the premium price is a barrier, thus making fair trade products the privilege of more well-to-do communities. Second, fair trade as it currently operates does not change the fundamental relationship between capital and labour. Capital still has the power to 'buy' labour and the fruits of labour. Paying a higher price will definitely alleviate the suffering of the producer, but Just Change is not about fair prices alone – it seeks to change the relation between capital and labour; between 'investors', producers and consumers. It is a structure that recognises that labour and capital both have roles to play in the economy but ensures that they are not in competition with each other but work in tandem for mutual benefit. Just Change is an alternative market system where all the actors – producers, consumers and investors – work collectively and for mutual benefit.

Beyond private ownership capital

The third theoretical leg of Just Change is rooted in more radical economics. In spite of the arguable collapse of capitalism during 2008, when governments had to step in with huge financial bail-outs to keep the system going, people still believe that capitalism in its present form is the only possible economic model. Just Change argues that by changing the role and function of financial capital we can create new economic models that result in a better distribution of wealth.

Based on research with the fishing community on the south-eastern coast of India, Just Change has developed a notion of 'participative capital'. In this mode, capital does not get ownership rights as it does in the present free market economy but only gets participant rights along with producers and consumers. In other words an 'investor' cannot automatically presume to 'own' any surpluses generated through the investment. The producer and consumer have equal claim to it because we argue that it was not the action of capital investment alone that resulted in the surplus. Producer 'investment', in the form of labour and the acceptance of a value for their produce that is lower than what the end consumer is willing to pay, and consumer 'investment', in the form of purchasing and consuming goods at a higher price than the actual cost of the product delivered to them, have both by their actions contributed to the surplus. Hence the division of that surplus has to be negotiated with all the three parties who have contributed to its generation.

Figure 13.1 shows that in traditional market capitalism model financial capital is invested to buy or hire physical capital like land and labour from households. This physical capital is used to create products that are then sold to households, generating a surplus or financial 'returns' on investment that belongs to the investor of capital, allowing the cycle to then repeat itself and ultimately resulting in increasing wealth accumulation in the hands of those who are capital rich.

The Just Change model in **Figure 13.2** shows that first of all the whole system is based on people (households) all participating in different forms. Financial capital does not 'buy' or 'hire' physical capital – and therefore does not get ownership rights as in the market capitalism model. Some people (investor households) participate by making money available for producer households, who use the money (**participative capital**) to create products that in turn are made available to other households, who participate by consuming these products (consumer households). Note that investor households also function as consumers. All surplus thus created belongs to all three actors. Wealth therefore does not accumulate only in the hands of the investors but is distributed among all participants.

This theoretical framework – where we seek to change the power relationships within a market economy – has led to setting up of Just Change as an international cooperative of producers, consumer and investors.

Figure 13.1: Market capitalism

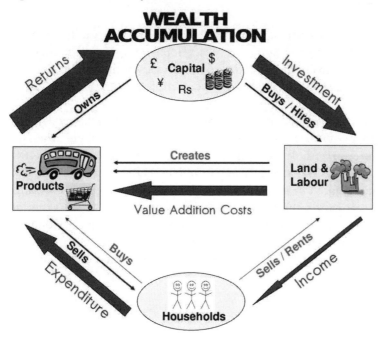

Figure 13.2: Participative capitalism

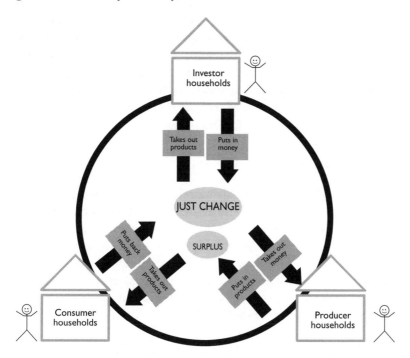

Operational framework

The challenge lies in operationalising this theoretical framework. In doing so Just Change has built on the community development work of the last few decades. Community groups have banded together to assert their rights, as in the case of the AMS, or in some cases purely for economic benefit, as in the case of microfinance groups.

Just Change works with such organised communities enabling them to enlarge their circle of solidarity to include other similar groups. For example, when the AMS as a producer of tea links up with the Social Agency for Women and Rural Development (SAWARD) in Kerala, who produce coconut oil (which AMS members consume), both groups benefit. In order to achieve this, Just Change has created two structures through which it operates in India. One is the Just Change Trust (JCT) and the other is the Just Change India Producer Company (JCIPC). Similar work is being undertaken in the UK and within Europe as well, and as a first step we have set up Just Change UK, which is a company limited by guarantee.

Just Change Trust

The Just Change Trust is a grant-based organisation that is registered under the Indian Trusts Act and is governed by a board of trustees. It recognises that if communities are to gain control of their economy and set up trading mechanisms they have to be supported to develop first an attitudinal shift – so that communities realise that collectively they are capable of taking control – and second the business skills needed for this. Thus JCT aims to develop the **social** and **human capital** of communities. It is unrealistic to expect that the cost of developing this can be recovered from the business alone. Therefore the Just Change Trust uses grant funding to support the development of social and human capital, which acts as the foundation for the deployment of financial capital.

Just Change India Producer Company

This company, unlike JCT, is a shareholder- or membership-based structure and is focused more on the deployment of financial capital to trade goods between its members. The company is governed by a board of directors representing all the member organisations and is managed by staff who are all chosen from within the community. Hence it is not grant based but 'investment' based. JCIPC has therefore to concern itself with things like profits, margins, rate of return, stock; it needs systems for procurement, for warehousing, for distribution and for retailing.

It was founded by four organisations:

- the Adivasi Munnetra Sangam (AMS) in Tamilnadu, which is the organisation of 3,000 Adivasi families;

- the Social Agency for Women and Rural Development (SAWARD), which is a federation of nearly 200 microfinance groups representing 2,000 women and their families, all living in a rural area just outside Kozhikode in Kerala;
- Bhoodhan Vikas Mandal (BVM), a group very similar to SAWARD, based in Nilambur, also in Kerala;
- Sahabaghi Vikas Abhiyan (SVA), which is the largest group of 40,000 families. It is a federation of a number of community groups representing Dalits and Adivasis in Western Orissa, one of the poorest areas of India.

The objectives of the company are:

- to ensure that both producers and consumers gain greater control and power in the market by establishing direct trading links between the two;
- to ensure that as much money as possible stays within the local economy;
- to ensure that when money has to flow out to purchase goods not produced locally it flows to other similar poor producer communities.

To do this the company has set up branches within each member organisation. Through these branches it has started village level shops called Village Consumer Societies. JCIPC attempts to first source products locally from the members of the organisation. For example, one of the village groups of SAWARD produces coconut oil. So all the oil sold in the SAWARD village shops is sourced from this group. However, if the product is not available locally then the company tries to source it from another member organisation. For example, tea is produced only by the AMS so it is sourced from the AMS and supplied to all the other member groups. If a product is not available within any of the groups then JCIPC sources it from other poor producers, even if they are not members of JCIPC. For example, rice is not grown by any of the member groups, so rather than buy it from the market JCIPC sources it directly from Aharam, which is a farmers' organisation in Tamilnadu. If a product is not available from these three sources it is then sourced from the open market. The aim, however, is to reduce sourcing products from the open market and source them directly from the three inner circles.

In the first year only 18% of JCIPC goods were sourced from the three inner circles and 82% was sourced from the open market. By 2009 60% was sourced from the three inner circles and only 40% from the open market. This means that initially for every pound sterling equivalent spent by a family all of it would flow out of the economy and into the 'market'. Today, 60 pence of this pound stays within the control of participating communities, where it recirculates and therefore has a multiplier effect (Sacks, 2002).

In the traditional market economy all the surplus generated would be 'owned' by the investor of financial capital. In the Just Change model the surplus is owned by all three actors – the producers, the consumers and the investors of capital. All are seen as contributing to the generation of surplus and so all have a share in the surplus and on terms that are decided by all. JCIPC taps into the **social**

capital and **human capital** developed by JCT to strengthen the local economy of its participating members.

While mainstream companies seek to increase financial profits, JCIPC seeks to increase 'social benefit'. This social benefit can take financial forms like lower costs to consumers and higher prices to producers but can also take other forms like more local jobs and more control over decision making. Hence the social return on investment is as important as financial return. In assessing our 'bottom line' we will measure both the financial gains as well as the social gains.

In keeping with its values, it is written into the constitution of JCIP that at all times the company will seek to arrive at decisions through consensus rather than voting. As a result of this culture of consensus, a lot of work has to go into keeping members sufficiently informed. This effort pays off, because decisions are therefore well informed and there is complete ownership over the decision – which is not necessarily the case when it is done through voting.

How is JCIPC funded?

When we launched Just Change we saw it only as a cooperative of producers and consumers. A friend and supporter of Just Change, Lord Joffe from the UK, challenged this model by saying "The producers and consumers you work with are themselves cash poor. How can they come up with the investment that might be needed?" We then went on to expand the model to include investors. Hence JCIPC, as mentioned earlier, is investment based and not grant dependent.

While developing the investment model, we discovered that producers and consumers can also be investors. Hence the first source of capital investment is from the members themselves. This comes in two forms: by the village putting up the working capital to run their village shops, and the member groups taking shares in the company. However, as these members are cash poor, what they put up is not likely to be sufficient. JCIPC is therefore creating financial instruments like Social Return Bonds (SRB) or Product Bonds that will allow people to invest in Just Change. A SRB is one where an individual or group invests in JCIPC and, rather than committing a financial return as is done in market capitalism, JCIPC commits to creating social benefit in forms described earlier. The 'investors' therefore know that their capital investment is continuously being used to create social benefit for poor communities. A Product Bond, on the other hand, will allow the investor to get a return but this will be in products rather than money. The idea is that people are 'investing' in long-term change and not just for financial advantage.

Just Change UK

Just Change is not about India alone. Ever since my wife and I visited the UK in 1994 to look at poverty and community work in the UK from a southern perspective, we maintained our links with a number of disadvantaged groups within the UK. It always troubled us that these communities could not afford fair trade products. We were keen that Just Change should include these groups. So we have set up Just Change UK (JC UK), a company limited by guarantee (www.justchangeuk.org). JC UK works primarily through volunteer groups in different cities who spread the Just Change concept through different networks, including faith groups, schools and community groups.

Marsh Farm Outreach, a community group on the Marsh Farm social housing estate in Luton, has joined the Just Change network. They have used the tea from India to set up a social enterprise through which they sell the tea to local residents, local shops and distribute in the South of England. Glenn Jenkins of Marsh Farm, describes Just Change as a system where 'everyone makes a living and no one makes a killing'.

Conclusion: what the future holds

We are now faced with the challenge of running a business with the efficiencies of a private sector market-based organisation coupled with the values and culture of the voluntary sector – our values and politics should dominate our economics and not the other way around. As we move into the future, we are exploring how to build Just Change into a much more robust system that is not so easily affected by the vagaries and greed of a market economy. One way forward is to develop our own currency. We hope to learn from the number of local currency initiatives being developed across the globe (Lee, 1996).

Another challenge we face will be our growth. As we grow larger can we retain the spiritual relationships and values with which we began? History tells us as organisations grow, rules replace relationships and a bureaucracy emerges that makes functioning through relationships very difficult. How can we deal with this? We have no ready-made answers.

But the essence of the model is its flexibility to respond to both local situations and changing situations. This flexibility requires us to be sensitive and willing to learn from other points of view. When Joel Joffe pointed out that we needed to bring investors into the model we were quick to learn and develop ways of doing this. This lies at the heart of all innovation and enterprise, especially when it seeks to bring about social change and justice.

Just Change is an attempt to achieve what the students gathered in the small town of Poonamallee on the outskirts of Madras declared way back in 1972, "We were born into an unjust society and we are determined not to leave it the way we found it."

References

Dees, G. (1998) *The meaning of social entrepreneurship*, Stanford, CA: Stanford University.

Lee, R. (1996) 'Moral money? LETS and the social construction of local economic geographies in South East England', *Environment and Planning*, vol 28, no 8, pp 1377-94.

Sacks, J. (2002) *The money trail: Measuring your impact on the local economy using LM3*, London: New Economics Foundation and the Countryside Agency.

Thekaekara, S. and Thekaekara, M. (1995) *Across the geographical divide*, London: Centre for Innovation in Voluntary Action.

FOURTEEN

Conclusion

Robert Gunn and Chris Durkin

In this book the editors have set out a three-stage vision of the different skills required to analyse, instigate, sustain and reflect on different aspects of social entrepreneurship. We have used this particular focus to examine how social enterprises have evolved in a UK policy context and explored the difficulties in defining organisations that can have diverse structures and pursue different aims. The one thing that seems to bind them all together is the desire, by social entrepreneurs, to pursue a social mission using an organisation that is funded sustainably.

We have expanded our investigation beyond the skills required to set up and run organisations to look at the realities that entrepreneurs face. While skills are essential and can be learned from attending courses or reading books, personal and professional reflection has also been shown to be important in the learning that has taken place among the entrepreneurs whose cases we have highlighted. Management of change is an important issue and learning by doing and reflecting on real outcomes in order to keep organisations viable and sustainable appears to be another key skill that entrepreneurs develop as they pursue their social missions.

We have chosen to focus on organisations that are located in a specific community and are generally small in organisational terms. We have seen that community and participatory approaches are important ways of identifying need, and in the process we have looked at the role of the individual and the community in which they are based and to which they relate directly. We have noted that individuals and organisations change over time and that sustainability is a key aspect of social enterprise when it is meets welfare needs that are not being met by the state or the market. There is almost a moral duty on entrepreneurs to consider how they will sustain a service if they have people who are dependent on them to improve their lives and social situations. This moral imperative is closely linked to the reflective aspects of an entrepreneur's development and daily practice. Being clear who the stakeholders are and how those in need can have a voice in keeping the organisations firmly focused on their aims is a challenging aspect of social entrepreneurship. The values and beliefs of stakeholders, entrepreneurs and other organisational partners will develop and mature during the life of organisations. While circumstances change, identifying core values and beliefs and using them to evaluate the social mission of social enterprises is important to prevent organisational drift. When reflecting, social entrepreneurs can ask themselves, does this organisation uphold the human rights of all those people involved in its activities?

Skills for policy analysis

Specifically, Buchanan has raised the difficult question of sustainability for organisations that may be economically insecure, in competition with the state sector, grant dependent and face a loss of a distinct place or identity in what has become known as the third sector. While the activities of entrepreneurs remain a vibrant source of social action, the legislative and policy context in which they operate are important aspects of their sustainability.

Kulothungan has helped us define what a social enterprise is in the context of a capitalist economic system. Importantly, social entrepreneurship crosses the traditional boundaries between government bureaucracy, voluntary association and private sector businesses. Social enterprise can draw from each of these worlds but is defined by higher levels of innovation and creativity than has generally been the case for organisations solely pursuing social aims.

Skills for social entrepreneurship

Bryant used a community development model to show the importance of working with real people to formulate the aims for a social project and the importance of ensuring stakeholders are central to evaluating the progress and viability of activities undertaken for social ends. He identified and explored some tools to assess need that can be used to benchmark and evaluate organisational activity.

Durkin and Gunn have shown us how to identify which people and organisations can have a stake in social enterprises so that entrepreneurs can identify the key players they will be relating to when they engage in practical social entrepreneurship. Although policy contexts define wider goals at governmental and regional levels, they are brought alive by individuals. Entrepreneurs need to know who these key individuals are and what power each of them may be able to exercise in the running of organisations. Durkin and Gunn give us an analysis of how power can work in such organisations.

With governments now supporting the growth of social enterprises and offering financial incentives for individuals to move beyond traditional state organisations and set up independent service provision, Urwin describes the different types of funding available and the advantages and disadvantages of the various methods of finance. The case studies demonstrate the different types of funding that entrepreneurs have drawn on when running their organisations, and how they have to manage a mix of financial instruments.

Ferguson provides an accessible model of financial planning and control to help aspiring entrepreneurs with an aspect of entrepreneurship that may not have been at the front of their minds when setting out on a social mission. Having money to bring aims to reality is essential if an organisation is to be successful.

Being able to control finance and respond rapidly to changing circumstances are key elements of entrepreneurship if it is to bring long-term benefits to people and communities.

Kulothungan's theme of innovation is explored in more detail by Curtis. The challenges and risks that pursuing an innovative approach can produce are placed against the moral and ethical dimensions inherent in organisations designed to fulfil a social purpose. Such purposes are seen to change and be very difficult to quantify.

Griffith looks at our theoretical understanding of management and leadership and shows us how these can be used by the entrepreneur to shape and direct social enterprises. Social aims can be difficult to achieve at the same time as being economically viable; this tension is another core aspect of the social entrepreneur's experience. Finance and financial management may be in conflict with social aims and the management of this double bottom line is challenging.

Skills in practice

This is where theory meets practice. The case examples in the book show how real entrepreneurs handle these tensions and the differences inherent in diverse cultural settings and the range of ways funding can be obtained to pursue social aims. Young helps us understand the core motivations for a first-time entrepreneur. She helps us understand how the raw emotions of experience are translated into social action and how the skills described in the earlier sections of the book are used to construct an organisation that meets those defining aims. Her reflection on what she has lived through and the lessons it has taught her define social entrepreneurship as a life-changing experience for practitioners and also for the people who benefit from their activities.

Sugden and Mendes have contextualised the state of social entrepreneurship in the US. The case example that they describe exemplifies the 'can do' spirit inherent in an economy rooted in the capitalist model. Entrepreneurs are shown to be tough and resilient people who can hold on to their sense of purpose in difficult and rapidly changing environments.

The example from China is interesting because it describes an organisation that does not rely on external sources of grant funding and is financially independent. So and Chyau take ideas from their US experience of business education and relocate them to a very different cultural setting. Their work emphasises how social commerce has become a global phenomenon and how market success within a global context may be seen to drive social improvement. Buchanan's early comments about sustainability and changing circumstance serve to remind us that while there are benefits in a market approach, there are also potential difficulties in sustainability when global economies are as volatile as has been our recent experience.

Finally Thekaekara's work gives a longitudinal perspective on the development and thinking behind the pursuit of social entrepreneurship in an Indian setting.

He reinforces the lessons to be learned from the volatility of market solutions and globalisation, but the thinking behind the featured social enterprise has moved beyond accepting the norms of traditional capitalist economies to the pursuit of economic models that may benefit the oppressed rather than the elite. He presents an analysis of change, in which the social enterprise has had to adapt to the changing needs of a community, while at the same time adjusting to a developing economic climate. It will be very interesting to see how these ideas develop. Perhaps we will return to them in later editions of this book.

Social entrepreneurship and social enterprise are now truly global phenomena playing a significant, albeit small, role in the world economy. Although a global phenomena, what is recognised as a social enterprise may be different in each country, reflecting history and culture, with a greater emphasis on profit in, for instance, the US model in contrast to the more community-oriented European model. What is at the core of each model, however, is the dual focus of social mission and profit. Their potential for good has to be balanced against the need for sustainability, a juggling act that can at times lead to 'organisational drift' and a focus on one aim to the detriment of the other.

We hope that this book provides readers with an understanding of what these issues really mean and the skills entrepreneurs need to bring their aspirations to life.

Internet resources

Although social entrepreneurship is a relatively new area of study, there are an increasing number of internet resources available. In this section we have identified a number of websites that we believe may be of help to both students and practitioners. Although many are UK based, we have identified a number from the US, some from Asia and others that have a more 'global' reach. Finally we have included a broad-based section that includes research centres, think tanks and foundations.

Policy and general resources

Because social entrepreneurs and social enterprises operate in all sectors of the economy it is sometimes difficult to categorise them. However, in the UK they are generally seen as being part of the third sector. In this section we have identified a number of links, in particular governmental and infrastructure organisations that offer advice support and training. Each one has links to other organisations and publications.

Coity Action Network – provides business support for social enterprises: www. can-online.org.uk

Community Interest Companies – substantial information about community interest companies: www.cicregulator.gov.uk

Development Trusts Association – describes itself as the leading network of community enterprise practitioners dedicated to helping people set up development trusts and helping existing development trusts learn from each other and work effectively: www.dta.org.uk

Improvement and Development Agency for local government – section on social enterprise and local government: www.idea.gov.uk/idk/core/page. do?pageId=8840188

Institute for Sommuncial Entrepreneurs – US-based organisation: www. socialent.org/

Know How Non Profit – UK-based site that aims to be 'the place for non-profit people to learn and share what they have learnt with others': www. knowhownonprofit.org/

National Council for Voluntary Organisations (NCVO) – UK-based organisation that supports the voluntary and community sector. A very extensive site with a great deal of information and resources: www.ncvo-vol.org.uk

Office of the Third Sector (Cabinet Office) – UK government website with specific section on social enterprises: www.cabinetoffice.gov.uk/third_sector/social_enterprise

School for Social Entrepreneurs – provides training for people interested in and working for social enterprises. Also contains a resources section: www.sse.org.uk

Social Enterprise Alliance – US organisation that 'is dedicated to building a robust social enterprise field': www.se-alliance.org/

Social Enterprise Coalition – UK's national body for social enterprises. Gives details of regional support organisations: www.socialenterprise.org.uk

Social Entrepreneurship Teaching Resources Handbook – developed by Ashoka's Global Academy for Social Entrepreneurship in partnership with Debbi Brock. Includes a global faculty directory with profiles of people engaged in social entrepreneurship teaching and research around the world: www.universitynetwork.org/handbook

Social Enterprise Training and Support – provides information and resources focusing on social enterprise training, support and publications: www.setas.co.uk

Social Firms UK – UK national support organisation for the development of the social firm sector. Includes an extensive resources section: www.socialfirms.co.uk

Key skills

In this section we have identified websites that may be of use both practically and developmentally. We have divided this section into four sections:

1. general business and management
2. business support and planning
3. finance and funding
4. social innovation.

General business and management

Business Balls – provides free ethical learning and a development resource for people and organisations: www.businessballs.com/

Business Open Learning Archive (BOLA) – business studies primer, with a great deal of interesting and useful information and material. Based at Brunel University, UK: www.bola.biz

Free Management Library – provides resources relating to leadership and management: http://managementhelp.org/

Mind Tools – online management and leadership training website: www. mindtools.com

Social Innovator – is a collaboration between the National Endowment for Science, Technology and the Arts (NESTA) and the Young Foundation and has been set up 'to bring together the people, experience and issues involved in designing, developing and growing new ideas that meet pressing unmet needs': www.socialinnovator.info/

Business support and planning

Barclay J. (2006) *Is it a good idea? A guide for charities considering new social enterprise activity*, London: Cass Buiness School: www.cass.city.ac.uk/cce/pdf_files/ socialenterprise-goodidea.pdf

Business Link – UK government support service for businesses with a specific section on setting up a social enterprise: www.businesslink.gov.uk/socialenterprise

Business Planning Guide to Developing a Social Enterprise – www. forthsector.org.uk/docs/New_BusPlanGuide.pdf

Charities Aid Foundation – a registered charity that works to create greater value for charities and social enterprises: www.cafonline.org/

Guide to writing a Business Plan – a good basic booklet which focuses on writing a business plan: www.sustainable-enterprise.org.uk/documents/business_plan_guide.pdf

Finance and funding

Acumen Fund – claims to be 'a non-profit global venture fund that uses entrepreneurial approaches to solve the problems of global poverty'. It has offices in the US, India, Kenya and Pakistan: www.acumenfund.org/

Community Development Venture Capital Alliance (CDVCA) – network for community development venture capital based in the US: www.cdvca.org/

'Financing your social enterprise' – Business Link information about how to finance social enterprises: www.businesslink.gov.uk/bdotg/action/detail?type=RESOURCES&itemId=1079871206

Guidestar – US non-profit organisational database: www2.guidestar.org/Home.aspx

GuideStar UK – comprehensive database about UK-based charities: www.guidestar.org.uk

Investors Circle – a network of investors, professional venture capitalists, foundations and others who are using private capital to promote the transition to a sustainable economy: www.investorscircle.net/

J4b – grant information for the UK and Ireland: www.j4b.co.uk

New Philanthropy Capital (NPC) – a consultancy and think tank which helps funders and charities to achieve a greater impact: www.philanthropycapital.org/

Social Edge – section on funding and support in Europe: www.socialedge.org/features/resources/funding/funding-and-support-europe

Social Investment Forum – US national non-profit membership association for professionals, firms and organisations dedicated to advancing the practice and growth of socially responsible investing: www.socialinvest.org/

Social Return on Investment (European network) – described as 'an informal group of people developing the use of social return on investment across Europe. The website is designed to provide information on SROI and its use across Europe and on resources to help people': www.sroi-europe.org/

Social innovation

Business Ethics Resources – articles and website links on business ethics: www.bola.biz/ethics/

Center for Social Innovation – based at Stanford Business School, its mission is 'to create ideas that deepen and advance our understanding of management and with those ideas to develop innovative, principled, and insightful leaders who change the world': http://csi.gsb.stanford.edu/

Change.org – an online hub for social change: www.change.org/ It has a specific section on social entrepreneurship: http://socialentrepreneurship.change.org/

Innovation Tools – claims to be the world's largest website focused on business innovation, creativity and brainstorming: www.innovationtools.com/

Intrapreneurship – Gifford and Pinchot's work: www.intrapreneur.com

Open University Open Learn Unit on Managing Complexity – a course that aims to develop skills of thinking systematically and creatively about issues of complexity: http://openlearn.open.ac.uk/course/view.php?id=3336&topic=all

Social Innovation Exchange – describes itself as 'a global community of individuals and organisations committed to promoting social innovation and growing the capacity of the field': www.socialinnovationexchange.org/

Wicked Issues – Jeff Conklin's work on wicked issues, and includes information about the **CogNexus Institute**, which aims to help people and organisations deal with complex and ill-structured situations: http://cognexus.org/index.htm

Asia

We have identified a number of useful websites whose focus is on the fast expanding social enterprise sector in Asia. Some of these websites contain extensive resource sections.

Avantage Ventures – advisory firm focusing on growing the social enterprise industry in Asia. It has a very extensive resources section with a directory of links to social enterprise resources both within Asia and globally: www.avantageventures.com

Just Change India – community-led initiative that 'seeks to regain power in markets by directly linking producers, consumers and investors in a network that is mutually beneficial': www.justchangeindia.com

Just Change UK – links communities in India and the UK: www.justchangeuk.org

National Social Entrepreneurship Forum – aims to promote social entrepreneurship and inspire, educate and support new social entrepreneurs among the youth in India: http://nsef-india.org/

Social Entrepreneurship Forum – a website set up by a 'group of like-minded individuals' interested in social entrepreneurship: www.seforum.sg/

Society for Research and Initiatives for Sustainable Technologies and Institutions – includes a section on social enterprises: www.sristi.org/

ThinkChange India – a leading source of information on social innovation and social entrepreneurship in India: www.thinkchangeindia.org/

UnLtd India – similar to the UK-based organisation in that it works with start-up social entrepreneurs: http://unltdindia.org/

Research

Research centres

Center for the Advancement of Social Entrepreneurship (CASE) – a research and education centre based at Duke University's Fuqua School of Business. It aims to promote the entrepreneurial pursuit of social impact through the thoughtful adaptation of business expertise: www.caseatduke.org/

EMES – describes itself as 'a research network of established university research centres and individual researchers whose goal is to gradually build up a European corpus of theoretical and empirical knowledge, pluralistic in disciplines and methodology, around "Third Sector" issues': www.emes.net/

Skoll Centre for Social Entrepreneurship – based at the Saïd Business School, University of Oxford, it describes itself as a leading global entity for the advancement of social entrepreneurship that aims to foster innovative and social transformation through education, research and collaboration: www.sbs.ox.ac. uk/centres/skoll/

Social Enterprise Initiative – based at the Harvard Business School, it 'aims to generate knowledge and to inspire, educate, and support current and emerging leaders in all sectors to apply management skills to create social value': www.hbs. edu/socialenterprise/

Social Enterprise Knowledge Network (SEKN) – a collaborative research network, where members share learning, participant-centered teaching and aim to strengthen management education of member institutions' capabilities to serve their communities: www.sekn.org/

Third Sector Research Centre – aims to 'bridge the gap' between research and the third sector. Although it is based at the University of Birmingham, it is in collaboration with the University of Southampton and includes contributions from Middlesex and Kent Universities. It is funded by the Economic and Social Research Council, Office of the Third Sector and Barrow Cadbury Trust: www. tsrc.ac.uk

University Network for Social Entrepreneurship – works with professors, researchers, practitioners and students to develop social entrepreneurship. It is designed to be a resource hub and an action-oriented discussion forum to expand social entrepreneurship education and participation around the world: www. universitynetwork.org/

Think tanks and foundations

Ashoka – claims to be the global association of social entrepreneurs, with contacts and offices on all continents: www.ashoka.org/

Demos – describes itself as interested in power and politics, in particular how to give people more power, and has published reports on social enterprises: www.demos.co.uk/

Leader to Leader Institute – aims to strengthen the leadership of the social sector: www.pfdf.org/

National Endowment for Science, Technology and the Arts (NESTA) – aims to make the UK more innovative. Interested in social innovation and social entrepreurship: www.nesta.org.uk

New Economics Foundation – independent think tank that aims to 'improve quality of life by promoting innovative solutions': www.neweconomics.org/

Schwab Foundation for Social Entrepreneurship – international foundation that aims to advance social entrepreneurship and to foster social entrepreneurs: www.schwabfound.org/

Skoll Foundation – describes its mission as being 'to drive large-scale change by investing in, connecting and celebrating social entrepreneurs and other innovators dedicated to solving the world's most pressing problems': www.skollfoundation.org/

Young Foundation – a UK centre for social innovation: www.youngfoundation.org/

UnLtd – describes itself as an online community of social entrepreneurs and support providers: www.unltd.org.uk

UnLtd World – aims to connect people to the 'tools and information you need to change the world. A world wide resource': www.unltdworld.com/

Index